BRIDGE BURNING
and OTHER HOBBIES

BRIDGE
BURNING
and OTHER HOBBIES

KITTY
FLANAGAN

ALLEN&UNWIN
SYDNEY · MELBOURNE · AUCKLAND · LONDON

Allen & Unwin
83 Alexander Street
Crows Nest NSW 2065
Australia
Phone: (61 2) 8425 0100
Email: info@allenandunwin.com
Web: www.allenandunwin.com

 A catalogue record for this
book is available from the
National Library of Australia

ISBN 978 1 76087 747 7

Illustrations by Tohby Riddle
Set in Fairfield LH by Midland Typesetters, Australia
Printed in Australia by McPherson's Printing Group

10 9 8 7 6 5 4 3 2 1

The paper in this book is FSC® certified.
FSC® promotes environmentally responsible,
socially beneficial and economically viable
management of the world's forests.

For Penny—my sister and my best friend

CONTENTS

Foreword from a witch's familiar   ix

PART ONE WHEN I WAS YOUNG AND OTHER CLICHÉS

Unbearable me   3
The Vardy Party   13
Yoga Guantanamo   21
'We cannot have tears because of maths'   29
The Wishbone Chicken Shop   41
Schnitzel and chips   51
The great wife swap   55
Grande dame at the dance   63

PART TWO HITCH-HIKING, OLDER MEN AND OTHER
              BAD DECISIONS

The fancy Fig   71
How am I not dead?   79
Earn 1000 Dollars a Week, Ask Me How!   85
Catchphrasey Joe   91

Two birds in a bunker   101

Drug talk   107

Bridge burning in Singapore   119

PART THREE THE GRAVEDIGGER'S WIFE, THE STONER'S
                PROSTITUTE AND OTHER FAILED ROMANCES

A bit of a dick   133

List Man   145

The Noble Arsehole   151

The Gravedigger's Wife   161

I love a bidet   173

A security guard, a typographer and a plumber
all walk into a bar   185

PART FOUR PUT LESS ON YOUR FORK, DON'T PARK ACROSS
                DRIVEWAYS AND OTHER THINGS I HAVE LEARNED

Black sofas and Pink Ladies   201

Food rules   209

Getting egged   217

Snow White—The early years   225

Comedian, heal thyself   235

The circle of life   243

Epilogue   253

Acknowledgements   257

FOREWORD
FROM A WITCH'S FAMILIAR

Babies are not like puppies. Puppies are usually delighted when I pick them up, and there is no such thing as an ugly puppy. Babies, on the other hand, are a complete lottery. That's what my parents discovered when they had me. I had a head that frightened even my own mother occasionally. It was large, bald and had two black holes in it. Those were my eyes, which were so dark you couldn't distinguish the iris from the pupil. I was also very small and I walked unnaturally early. Remember that creepy, dancing baby thing from early internet times? I think it may have been modelled on me. Imagine that walking in on you while you were having a shower or taking a pee. That's what my poor mother had to contend with on a daily basis. And that's also how things stayed until I was almost two years old.

Mum freely admits she used to find me, her own child, slightly sinister. Apparently it was the way I would stare at her and follow her around the room with my beady eyes to the point where (probably after a few drinks, it was the late sixties after all, who didn't enjoy a gin and tonic while breastfeeding?) she was convinced she'd given birth to a witch's familiar. That's right, my own mother says there were times when she worried that she'd given birth to a minor demon who worked as a witch's servant.

I don't find this offensive by the way. Rather, I think it defines what a terrific parent my mother was always going to be. It was clear from the start she was never going to suffer from parental blindness, she would always be able to see when her own kids were not the brightest, the most beautiful or the most well-mannered little angels who could do no wrong and I think that's important. It's largely thanks to my mother's no-

nonsense parenting style that this book is not an autobiography. Had I told my mother I was writing an autobiography, she'd quite rightly have asked, 'Why?' Instead, this is a book of true stories and ill-informed opinions. And I believe it was Paul Simon who once said, 'Your opinion is not important, it is merely of interest.' So, while this book is not important, I do hope you will find it of interest. Most of all,

I hope you will find it funny because that really is my favourite thing. I am almost ashamed to admit how much I love getting a laugh—for me, it is still the ultimate high. Admittedly, I don't take a lot of drugs.

Kitty Flanagan
January 2018

PART ONE

WHEN I WAS YOUNG AND OTHER CLICHÉS

UNBEARABLE ME

When I was young, I wanted to be Jodie Foster. Sometimes I wanted to be Kristy McNichol, but mostly I wanted to be Jodie Foster. How fun was her life? Shooting marshmallow guns in *Bugsy Malone*, tricking her parents in *Freaky Friday* and being an underage prostitute in *Taxi Driver*. I often thought, wow, that could have been me, because Jodie and I had very similar origin stories in that we both got our show business start in commercials.

Before Jodie was on TV and in films, she was a cute three-year-old in a Coppertone ad. It was one of a series of commercials that used the tagline 'Don't be a Paleface' and featured a dog pulling down a toddler's bikini bottoms to expose her little white bum. Can you imagine that ad being made today? Not only would that dog be in jail for inappropriate behaviour, but social media would be in overdrive trying to shame a three-year-old for not slip, slop, slapping.

People would post things like:

'Hey @jodiefosterage3, obviously you want all kids to get skin cancer and die! I hope YOU get skin cancer and die.'

'Nice one @jodiefosterage3, so you think being mauled by a dog is funny. I hope YOU get mauled by a dog and die.'

Obviously those comments are fabricated, if they were real, there'd be no punctuation and the word mauled would be spelled 'mawlled'.

Point is, I'm sure I could have had a brilliant, Oscar-winning Hollywood life, just like Jodie, if only my pesky parents hadn't insisted on my being so ordinary.

At three years old, I was a 'confident' child—and by 'confident' I mean that if it wasn't for my mother being eternally vigilant about manners and 'tone', I'd have been an unbearable, cheeky little shit.

I'd also finally grown some hair and no longer looked like a miniature Uncle Fester. In fact I was fairly cute—most kids are at that age. It's also when most of us peak in the looks department. You can't beat a chubby little face, a button nose and sweet little baby teeth for aww factor. The difference between me and every other cute kid, however, was that I had a dad who worked in advertising. This was the seventies and getting cast in ads was less about agents and more about who you knew in the business. Nepotism ruled.

This is how I like to imagine my casting went down.

Everyone at the ad agency comes back from a big, boozy, *Mad Men*-type lunch and then someone remembers, 'Shit, isn't there a shoot tomorrow? Weren't we supposed to organise a kid? Did anyone organise a kid?'

'What sort of kid?'

'A girl one. Actually, I don't care, if you can find me a decent-looking boy, we'll stick a wig on him and hope no one notices, just get me a kid.'

Following this exchange, some half-pissed art director starts wandering around to people's offices shouting, 'Hey? Does anyone have a kid? I need a kid for a shoot, does anyone have one? We need a kid. We're shooting tomorrow?'

My dad, tired of the shouting, calls back, 'How old?'

Pissy Art Director says, 'God, I don't know . . .' he thinks for a minute then holds his hand about two and a half feet above the ground, 'About this old . . .? How old's that? Two? Seven?'

Turns out it was three and that's how I came to 'star' in an ad for a very special type of fabric called Viyella. If you're not familiar with Viyella, it's an ingenious material which blends merino wool with cotton. That's right, all the warmth of wool plus the comfort of cotton. 'Why on earth are we not all still wearing Viyella?' I hear you ask, 'It sounds sublime!' And it sure does. It's probably because these days, we prefer to buy clothes made for a dollar, cut from appalling synthetic fibres that start to stink the minute they get near your armpit and then fall apart after a few wears. What happened to our standards?

Anyway, I was to be the face of Viyella. Even now I'm incredibly pleased with my three-year-old self. What a terrific decision, associating myself with a quality product like Viyella. Even social media wouldn't have been able to fault me.

'OMG! Viyella has changed my life, so comfortable, thanks @kittyflanaganage3! I hope you never die.'

Actually, that's unlikely, no doubt there would have been some blowback from the wool industry.

'Hey @kittyflanaganage3, what's wrong with pure wool? Blended fibres are unAustralian. Thanks for ruining our industry you sheep-hater. I hope you die.'

I should say at this point that I have absolutely no recollection of the shoot itself. I just remember Mum telling me all about it a few years later when I found a photograph of me and this very glamorous dark-haired woman in matching dresses. I asked Mum who the woman was and that's when I heard the story of Viyella and Pretend Mummy, aka the model who'd been hired to play my mother. (In fairness, I'm pretty sure she was hired first and I was hired to play her daughter.)

I do remember wondering why my own mother didn't play my mother in the ad. For a start, she looked a lot more like me than the woman in the photo, and also, I thought my mum would have looked more like a normal person when she laughed. The woman in the photo had her head tilted back and her mouth open in a weird phoney way that didn't look like real laughing. My mum could easily have replaced this woman, she was young and seventies glam, she'd popped out her kids early and played a lot of tennis. These days, she'd have been one of those annoying women in magazines who say things like, 'How I got my bikini body back in just six weeks!' Only she'd have no tips to share on how she did it because she did nothing. She just had her kids when she was young. That's the real secret. Get pregnant when your body is still like rubber!

Knowing my mother a lot better now, I totally understand why they hired a model. If they'd asked Mum to be in the ad (and they may well have) I know for a fact she'd have laughed in their faces and said, 'I'd rather be dead.'

My mum is not impressed at all by show business or television or parading around on stages shouting, 'Look at me, look at me!' which is a fairly accurate description of what I do for a job. It's just not her thing. She sees it for exactly what it is—a fun but pretty lightweight way to make a living. And hats off to her for knowing how to keep it real before the concept of keeping it real was even invented. It's very easy to stay grounded and not get 'up yourself' when you have a mother like mine.

Back on the Viyella set, my job was simple. All I had to do was run into Pretend Mummy's open arms and get a hug. Awwww. The technique they used to achieve this was similar to the one you'd employ in order to make a dog come when you call it. They lured me with a treat. The only difference was they used sugar instead of liver.

Someone grabbed my collar (the little peter pan one on my dress, in case you were misled by the dog analogy and thought they had me tethered with a collar and lead) and held me just out of frame. My Fake Mummy stood with her arms outstretched towards me, waiting to receive me and wrap me up in a big fake hug! Meanwhile, Real Mummy stood behind Fake Mummy, just out of shot, waving a lolly above Fake Mummy's head. And that was all it took.

The director called action, or possibly 'Release the idiot!' and the idiot ran full pelt at Fake Mummy. Only of course I wasn't running towards Fake Mummy, I was racing like a crazed Boxing Day shopper at the sugary treat Real Mummy was waving above Fake Mummy's head. Fake Mummy would then hug me nice and tight, pinning my arms to my sides. If she hadn't done that, the shot would have been me reaching for and clawing at the lolly above her head. As it was, I never once took my eyes off the prize. My 'eyeline', as they call it in the biz, was always way above Fake Mummy's head rather than where it should have been, gazing fake lovingly into her eyes.

The minute the director called cut, I'd thrash around in Fake Mummy's arms, desperate to get my arms free and claim my reward. See what I mean? Training a dog and training a kid, there's really not that much difference.

By all accounts I was fabulous in this ad. Everybody said so. Everyone was very happy, the client, the director, Fake Mummy, the advertising people—everyone except Real Mummy and Real Daddy. They maintain that one day on a film set turned me into a complete and utter turd overnight, which is why they kyboshed any further requests for my 'cute kid' services.

My mother said it wasn't healthy to stand around all day being told you're beautiful. She said Fake Mummy and everyone else went on waaaaay too much about how pretty and fabulous I was. Being only three years old, I was programmed to believe what grown-ups told me and they were telling me I was pretty and fabulous. In short, I was pretty fabulous.

At this point I'd like to give props to my mother. She was a stay-at-home mum but she was also a rockin' seventies feminist. She knew it was sending a bad message to focus so intently on a little girl's looks, so she stepped in and shut that shit down.

Having got back into the business decades later, as an adult, and now having worked on sets with children myself, I can see what a slippery slope the child star thing is. It's hard working with kids, you don't want to upset them because time is money and an upset kid is an expensive kid. It's also notoriously difficult to coax a good performance out of a child. You can't get cranky when they get it wrong, over and over and over again. You can't yell at them, that certainly won't help, so what do you do? Well, you praise the bejesus out of them, that's what. Even when they're absolutely awful, you praise every little thing they do in a bid to encourage them and give them confidence. Mostly you do this so you don't upset them. So, basically, all a child actor hears all day is how fabulous they are, from everyone. Whether they are doing things right or wrong, it's all great, it's all fabulous!

On top of this there are often rewards or bribes thrown into the mix. Even when they are totally useless, mumbling their way through scenes, forgetting their lines, looking the wrong way and even stopping mid-take to say, 'Can I have McDonald's for lunch?' they are still told how brilliantly they are doing and rewarded with all manner of praise and treats. Any dog trainer will tell you that giving treats for bad behaviour only serves to reinforce the bad behaviour, so it's a wonder that any child actor actually goes on to have a career.

Despite my parents being so quick to cut my acting and modelling career short, literally after one day, they were still forced to invest a lot of time in what I like to call 'Bashing the showbiz turd out of me'.

Apparently after that one day on a commercial, I was addicted to the lens. Any time I saw a camera come out, I'd race to get in front of it. To me, a camera meant it was time to be fabulous and being fabulous was my new special skill. By all accounts I was a nightmare, I would push my sister out of the way and strike a pose like I was going to be on the cover of *Turdy Toddler Monthly*.

I've seen pictures of myself taken shortly after the Viyella shoot where I have both hands on my hips, with one hip kicked out to the side and—worst of all—I am really eyeballing the camera with alarming intensity. If I didn't know any better, I'd say I was trying to 'smeyes', which if you're not familiar with the term, means smiling with your eyes. I think Tyra Banks of *America's Next Top Model* fame coined the word.

After a stand-up show, I sometimes do photos with audience members and I recently went through a phase where I tried a bit of smeyesing. I don't usually get to see these photos, people snap them on their phones then go home without showing me. Recently someone very politely asked if I would like to 'check the photo' and I finally saw how weird and creepy my amateur smeyesing technique made me look. I would like to apologise to any member of the public who had their photo taken with me during my smeyesing phase. You are no doubt stuck with a photograph where you look completely normal but I look like I've been goosed with a Paddle Pop right before the pic was taken. Not goosed with a Paddle Pop *stick* you understand but the whole ice cream. My eyes are opened unnaturally wide and I look completely taken by surprise, as you would be if someone just shoved a freezing cold Paddle Pop up your arse.

I've also tried looking 'fee-yarce'—another Tyra Banks invention—in photos. My looking 'fee-yarce' phase was no better. Again, I'm sorry if you got stuck with a photo of you and me when I was in my 'fee-yarce' phase. In these pics I am squinting slightly but only with my right eye. I look worried that someone *might* be about to goose me with a Paddle Pop so I am clenching my bum tight as if to say, 'Hey! Keep out! No more ice creams up the arse! I'm done with that. Seriously!'

My parents dealt with this camera obsession of mine by refusing to take any photos of me. For a whole year. My dad, a prolific photographer, would snap the lens cap on and put his camera away if I came anywhere near the photo being taken. The upshot is there is an entire twelve months of family photographs where I am missing and my sister looks like she is an only child. It was her finest hour, she's never looked happier.

THE VARDY PARTY

In kindergarten, I ran with a bad crowd. The local primary school had a numbers problem, they needed more students in order to keep a certain number of teachers. Parents of kids who were 'borderline' age, like me, were actively encouraged to send their kids to school early rather than holding them back to start the following year. Which is how I came to start school at age four when most other kids were five. This is in stark contrast to today's enrolment trend, which is to hold your child back as long as possible in order to give him or her 'an edge' over the other students. It's the reason we now see kindergarten kids the size of walruses schlepping around the playground.

Besides being younger than everyone else, I was also a very small four-year-old, so in my kindergarten school photo, surrounded by five-year-olds, I look like I am off in the distance, despite being right next to everyone else.

Being such a runt, I was easily influenced by normal-sized children like Stella Vardy, who was what my mother described as a 'bold girl'. Stella Vardy feared no one, not even the teachers, whom she backchatted with alacrity. She also flashed her fanny at boys and threatened to flash everyone else's fanny at the boys too. You had to watch Stella, she was wily like a fox, always cosying up to you being all chummy but it was only so she could lure you in close enough to whip around and pull your pants down as soon as there was a big enough crowd.

However, the most impressive thing of all about Stella Vardy was that she defiantly threw her fruit in the bin every single lunchtime.

Even in kindergarten everyone knew you couldn't throw your fruit in the bin, it was one of those things you just didn't do, like cutting nice coloured pictures out of an encyclo-paedia for your school project or writing your own initials in wet cement (der!). Fruit stayed in the bottom of your bag for your mother to find at a much later date, mouldy and barely recognisable. No one said you had to eat the fruit but you absolutely could not toss it out. Throwing fruit in the bin was the schoolyard equivalent of a prisoner flipping his full meal tray on to the floor, in front of the guard, and saying, 'I'm not eating this shit. What are you going to do about it?'

I bet a lot of teachers at our school wished it was a prison, then they could have thrown Stella in the hole for a few days of solitary.

Rumour had it that Stella's father was a Vietnam veteran. I have no idea whether this is true or not. And I'm not exactly sure when I heard that rumour but I imagine it was after I left school. I don't think it would have meant much to me in kindergarten. I certainly don't recall standing around the monkey bars tipping off all the other kids with advice like, 'Alright guys, word is Ol' Man Vardy is a Vietnam vet so I guess we'd better be careful this weekend at Stella's birthday party. Don't anybody mention the war!'

Which, of course, would have been followed by laughs and guffaws from all the five-year-old *Fawlty Towers* fans at my primary school.

Going to Stella Vardy's house was always a nerve-wracking experience. I remember the first time I went there with a few other girls for a sleepover. At bedtime, all five of us lay on the floor in sleeping bags and there was much giggling and squealing and a lot of shushing. Shushing that is always far louder than the actual talking. So it was just your typical, five-year-old girl carry on. Some time after lights out, the bedroom door opened and silhouetted in the doorway was the notorious Colonel Vardy* brandishing a long leather belt and telling us

---

* Note, I have no idea for sure that Mr Vardy was even in the army, let alone what rank he was and, as for notorious, how on earth would I know? I've never had access to his possibly non-existent military file.

to, 'Shut up and keep it down or we would all of us get the ruddy strap.'

I almost weed myself right there in the sleeping bag. I had never been hit with anything in my life, let alone a 'ruddy strap'.

After the Colonel slammed the door closed and once she was sure he'd walked away, Stella quickly laid out the extremely complicated Vardy household toilet rules. She whispered that if we had to go to the loo in the middle of the night, we mustn't *flush* the toilet because that would make a noise and it might wake her dad up and if that happened we'd all of us get the ruddy strap. I nearly weed myself again. My god, so much ruddy strapping in this house. The complication with not flushing, however, was that Mrs Vardy found unflushed wee disgusting. So, if you *did* pee during the night, you had to make sure you got up early in the morning to go and flush it before *Mrs* Vardy went into the bathroom and was greeted by the offensive sight of your unflushed wee. No doubt, in the Vardy household, not flushing would be yet another ruddy strappable offence.

What all of this boiled down to was that there was essentially a half hour flushing window between 6.30 a.m., when Mr Vardy left for work, and 7 a.m., when Mrs Vardy got up to take a shower. I remember drifting into a very fitful sleep invaded by images of Colonel Vardy lurking outside the bathroom with his ruddy strap and Mrs Vardy peering into the toilet shouting, 'Who did this wee?!!! Was it you, Kitty Flanagan? It looks like exactly the sort of wee you would do! Bring me the ruddy strap!' At least three of us had to go to the toilet that night. Small wonder that all the creeping around didn't provoke some sort of PTSD flashback. I just thank god none of us was wearing black pyjamas. Who knows what would have happened if Vardy thought there were Vietcong hiding out in his dunny.

Obviously, after such a harrowing experience, you would think no one would ever go to Stella's house again. But the problem was, you couldn't refuse Stella Vardy, or she'd pull your pants down for sure. Which is why no one had the nerve to say, 'No thank you, Stella, I don't want to come to your birthday party where there will be fun games like "Pin the ruddy strap on the donkey" and "What's the time, Mr Wolf? Is it flushing time or not flushing time?"'

So, at 2 p.m. that fateful Saturday afternoon in 1974, I headed off to Stella Vardy's Pardy.

This was the bygone age of children's parties when parents used to dump their kids and run, grateful to have an afternoon to themselves. Not like now where they hover around in case . . . in case . . . well I don't really know why they hang around. In case there's a child molester lurking in the Wendy House? In case there's gluten lurking in the birthday cake? In case their child decides they're having too much fun and doesn't ever want to return to their own home where the helicopter parents live?

It was also the era when little girls dressed like little girls rather than like miniature tramps working the back streets of The Cross. It was all long dresses, often homemade, and frilly socks and patent leather shoes. My mother had gone to the trouble of buying a pattern and some fabric and making me a special party dress. Cream cotton (possibly seersucker) printed all over with light pink roses, it had puffy sleeves and a hemline to the ankle—it really was a triumph. Teamed with a pair of shiny red buckle-up shoes, it was easily the last time I ever left the house shooting a couple of finger guns at myself in the mirror and thinking, *Flanagan, you are looking GOOOOOOD!!!*

The most exciting thing about any birthday party, apart from having *the* best dress ever, was the food. Junk food used to be a scarce commodity reserved for special occasions, which is why birthday parties were such a treat. Also it used to be quite common, and totally understandable, for parents to limit the number of kids invited. So there might only be eight invitations issued—unlike today where everyone in the whole class is invited. Which is just plain stupid.

Quite the sugar junkie, I made a beeline for the food table and began planning the afternoon's eating program. Fairy bread, pass. Mrs Vardy was way too liberal with the margarine and way too stingy with the hundreds and thousands—always disappointing when adults couldn't get a simple thing like that right. Also, bread is too filling which leaves less room for other treats.

The first thing any sensible child did when they got to a party was go straight to the Cheezels bowl and pop one cheesy orange ring on every finger—the equivalent of junk food insurance. You were then free to roam around the table enjoying everything else without worrying that the Cheezels might run out before you got your share. Ten fingers meant you had ten Cheezels in the bank.

Once my fingers were fully cheezeled, I moved up to the cocktail frankfurt bowl and started poking those things into my mouth as fast as I could dip them in the red sauce. How on earth they make horse nostrils and sawdust so damn tasty is a mystery, but hats off to Huttons.

With a double-dipped frank (no rules back then) halfway into my mouth, I watched as Stella Vardy's 2iC, Cindy Nolan (another bold girl/fanny flasher), arrived in a swathe of green chiffon. I'd always been quite taken with Cindy, and that day was no exception. She looked just like Hollywood Starlet Barbie. Gorgeous . . . but not *as* gorgeous as the plate of party sausage rolls being brought out to the table! Oh, it was heaven. So many fantastic foods, such a variety of mystery meats.

As I stood blowing on my too-hot sausage roll, sipping on a cup of dark-green G.I. cordial, loving myself sick and thinking the five-year-old equivalent of 'Life doesn't get any better than this', suddenly my life *did* get better when a voice behind me said, 'Gosh, isn't that a lovely dress.'

All too aware of the loveliness of my dress, I spun around and said, 'Thank you very much, my mum made it. From a *pattern!*' At which point I came face to face with Mrs Vardy's large arse and realised my error. She wasn't talking to or about me. She was one of the many who were paying tribute to Cindy Nolan, who was slowly but constantly revolving, like a pop-up ballerina in a jewellery box, so that everyone could admire her.

I quickly turned back to the food table, not caring, thinking no one had noticed my mistake and, far more importantly, there was still an entire plate of party sausage rolls right in front of me, so I planned to just keep on munching, no harm done. However, for some reason I will never understand, Mrs Vardy chose to openly mock my misunderstanding. She bent down and put her big ruddy face in mine and said, 'Oh!' Laugh laugh. 'Did you think we were talking to you, dear?' 'No, no, we were talking to Cindy! Her father brought her dress back from America!' The derisive laughter echoed around the room like something out of a seventies sitcom.

I thought by recounting this event, it might become clearer to me exactly why Mrs Vardy delighted in making such a public mockery of me. But I'm still none the wiser. Maybe some other kid did a wee in her precious toilet and didn't flush it and she suspected it was me. Maybe Stella told her I was the one who liked flashing my fanny at all the boys, that I was the bold girl who was the bad influence on everyone. Or maybe Mrs Vardy just didn't like me, which is fair enough. Sometimes a child is just unlikeable.

YOGA GUANTANAMO

I came to yoga well before it was a thing, I was only eight years old, so I was a very early adopter. I would have been considered quite the 'influencer', only there was no Instagram back then so I couldn't post pictures of my eight-year-old self warrior-posing it up on a clifftop.

Yoga was a very different beast when I was a child. It hadn't yet been embraced by celebrities or 'yummy mummies'. (I apologise for using that term. I find it quite the oxymoron. Do you know what's yummy? Hot chips. Do you know what's not yummy? Women in lycra pants with sweat stains around the box and crack. I know they're comfortable and it's a woman's right to choose comfort over style, but I'm not sure I'd want to go out with a guy who wore tracksuit pants all day every day because they were comfortable. Fair's fair, ladies.)

The only people who did yoga in the seventies were zealots, proper yogis and Hare Krishna types, and it was among people like this that I first experienced yoga. On the Easter holiday weekend my mother sent me off to yoga camp at Mangrove Mountain—an ashram slash commune slash place-to-go if you'd spent the sixties hanging out totally off the grid in India. That's how hard core these people were, they were off the grid before there was even a grid to be off. Admittedly, not all of them had spent time in India, some had just taken enough acid to *believe* they'd spent time there—in fact it's possible some of them had taken so much acid they thought Mangrove Mountain *was* India.

I've since asked my mother why on earth she sent me to a camp at this whack-job cooperative and she replied simply because she thought I would have fun. And in her defence, the pamphlet didn't describe it in the same way I have. Also, I was partially responsible. I was very keen to attend yoga 'camp'—the word 'camp' being the operative reason. I'd read a lot of books and seen a few movies where American kids went off to 'Summer Camp' and it seemed like great fun. Also, full disclosure, our family was Catholic and I'd worked out that the dates for camp would mean getting out of going to church, not just once but twice. Easter was a real downer of a holiday for Catholic kids. Yes you got four days off, but on at least two of those days you had to go to Mass.

So I went off quite willingly to Mangrove Mountain, thinking I'd really pulled the wool over my church-going mother's eyes and waving at my sister thinking, *Enjoy Mass, sucker! I'm going to camp to have the best fun ever! Say hello to God for me!*

Turns out the Catholic God is a vengeful god because yoga camp was hell on earth. The only way it vaguely resembled any movie about summer camp was if the movie was an old Western. This place was hot, dry and dusty. There were no trees, no grass, no bitumen, no concrete, just dusty dirt everywhere. Apart from the dust, everything was minimal. Sleeping quarters were rooms with dusty floors lined with bare bunks. You had to take your own sleeping bag. There was a thin yoga mat on each bunk bed which pulled double duty as exercise mat and may-as-well-not-even-be-there mattress. And that's because yoga wasn't about 'wellness and mindfulness' in the seventies, it was all about sacrifice and suffering.

This camp was the polar opposite of what I'd imagined. Instead of fun American-style camp counsellors called Chuck and Betty-Jo there were dour orange-robed yogis with top knots and names that were too long to remember and rhymed in a way that made them sound more like a doo-wop chorus than a name. Things like, Pramanama Bingbang and Shamalama Naknok. And that's not racist because as far as I can remember, none of them was actually Indian. All of them, however, thought we were a bunch of over-indulged Western kids who needed to learn how to live without the many trappings of modern society. Starting with meat. Going without meat isn't such a big deal these days, everyone knows vegetarian food can be delicious and that it has less impact on the planet and so accordingly, we say thumbs up to vegetarians. But back then, vegetarianism was pretty kooky and the only way most people knew how to cook vegetarian was to make standard meat and three veg then remove the meat from the plate.

At the ashram they were ahead of the game and had totally mastered vegetarian cooking. Here is their signature Mangrove Mountain recipe should you ever want to try it.

Ingredients
15 kg vegetables

15 litres water

1 kg turmeric*

Method
Place vegetable chunks into industrial-sized pot. Cover with plenty of water. Stir in turmeric. Boil for several hours.

* Cook's note: It is not possible to overdo the turmeric. If in doubt, add another fistful.

The yellow vegetable slop that resulted from this recipe was served up three times a day at yoga camp, including at breakfast, which blew my tiny eight-year-old mind. A mélange of vegetables for breakfast? I didn't even eat vegetables for dinner. In fact I didn't even eat vegetables when they were recognisable as vegetables or had individual identifiable colours like green and orange and white. And now here I was, being served the same ochre sludge three times a day. Breakfast was the same as lunch was the same as dinner. And good on them for their meticulous recycling. Nothing got scraped into the bin at Camp Goodtimes, anything left on our plates got scraped back into the main pot for the next meal.

I can see the point they were trying to make, that we were incredibly lucky to have any sort of food at all, let alone three times a day. How dare we expect variety. It was basically three days of being told, 'There are children starving in the world you ungrateful, spoiled little shits. Eat what you're given and be thankful to Swami Whatsernami for providing this bounty.' It's not a bad message, I'm just not sure I was ready to receive it at age eight. Or possibly there was a better way to pass on that message rather than through punishment and making us feel like arseholes for not being starving Indian children from the slums.

My solution was to become a starving Australian child and simply not eat for three days. And just so you know, there was zero risk of this ever happening. For several reasons. Firstly, I cannot *not* eat. Remember the 40 Hour Famine we used to all do when we were kids, to raise money? I don't. For me, it was always the 4 Hour Famine. That's as long as I ever lasted.

Once, as a teenager, my mum served up a dinner I didn't like and I petulantly told her I wasn't going to eat it and that I would probably starve. My mother scoffed and said, 'Fine with me, go ahead and starve.' I got very dramatic then and accused her of wanting me to get anorexia. I'm not sure my mother has ever laughed harder. 'Oh have a go,' she said. 'Let's see you get anorexia.' She wasn't a bad mother, she just knew there was no way I would ever stop eating.

I wasn't going to starve at yoga camp either, not because I'd force myself to eat the slurry, but because I had a secret food stash. Mum had given me a little half egg carton of six chocolate Easter eggs. Driven by starvation and despite promises to my mother that I would wait until Easter Sunday to open them, I decided to crack the carton early. My plan was to ration the eggs, one for breakfast, one for lunch, one for dinner etc. That would see me through until Easter Sunday at least.

Unfortunately, as I have already mentioned, I have an unholy addiction to sugar and the notion that I could ration chocolate was delusional. I ate all six eggs on Good Friday morning and, for a brief moment, it looked like the impossible might happen and I might actually starve. Then, on Saturday morning, the yogis brought out a whole box of red apples. The most delicious things I'd ever seen in my life. And though we were only supposed to have one each, I took six and hid them in my sleeping bag. These I could definitely ration out. Fruit is traditionally much easier to resist than chocolate.

Sadly, I wasn't the only kid who saw the apples and thought, Ahh! Finally! Food I recognise. Something not sloppy and yellow!

The box of apples was empty by the end of breakfast and the yogis were furious. They announced they would search every bag in order to expose the greedy Western ingrates who had taken more than one apple. I think I came close to fainting. Not since the threat of the Ruddy Vardy Strap back in '74 had I been so scared. The yogis proceeded to raid our room the way they do on TV prison shows, tipping the contents of bags out all over the floor, leaving kids scrabbling to rehome their possessions. Fortunately beds weren't searched, they didn't bother flipping our wafer-thin yoga mat mattresses, so my sleeping-bag apples remained undiscovered. Others weren't so lucky and as apples were turned up, individuals were led away to be punished. Many of them were crying because we all knew that the punishment would probably be 'The Well'.

The Well was all anyone could talk about at camp. Rumour had it that kids who did naughty things or disobeyed the 'Head Robe' at Mangrove Mountain were held by their ankles and dangled headfirst into The Well. Whether this actually happened or not, I don't know. I certainly never witnessed it. But the rumour was enough to keep us all petrified. One of the older boys at camp claimed he'd been held in The Well. And back then I totally believed him. Now I'm not so sure. I mean, really? Who would dangle a kid in a well? Surely even those humourless yogis had their limits.

Or maybe they didn't. In 2016, the Mangrove Mountain Ashram of the seventies and eighties—Australia's first ever ashram—was exposed as a cultish den of child sex abuse. To be clear, I neither experienced or witnessed any abuse of any kind, I just had a bad time at yoga camp because I didn't like vegetables, or yellow, or the grown-ups in charge who were mean and scary. Plus I really didn't like getting up at 6 a.m. if there was no television to watch. I was happy to get up every morning at 6 a.m. when I was at home but that was so I could watch *Thunderbirds*! At yoga camp, we had to get up and dutifully file into the yoga room to watch the Head Robe tip a teapot full of hot water up his nose, all of us terrified that we might be next. What if we got called up to the dais and had to have the teapot stuck up our nose? These days, I'd be happy to give it a crack, probably clear me out quite nicely, but at eight? The idea that someone was going to tip a teapot of water up my nose was akin to the threat of waterboarding.

After three days at Yoga Guantanamo, we were put on the train and sent back to Central Station. Mum, Dad and Penny were all there to greet me as I got off the train and I'll never forget the experience of crying when I saw them. I didn't know then that it was possible to cry with joy or relief. All I knew was there were tears streaming down my face but I wasn't sad. I was so confused, I kept saying to my mum, 'I'm not sad, I'm so happy. I'm so happy.'

Then I remembered to ask the most important question, 'Did you go to church already?'

Turned out they'd decided to wait so we could all go to Sunday evening Mass as a family. Unfuckingbelievable. After all I'd endured that weekend and I still had to go to Mass.

That's when I learned one of life's most important lessons. There is no God.

'WE CANNOT HAVE TEARS BECAUSE OF MATHS'

I have never been great at maths. Actually, that's an overstatement. I've never even been good at maths. Except for my one golden patch in year eleven when I aced a maths exam, got 98 per cent and suddenly found myself streamed into the top maths class. When I say, 'I aced the exam' what I mean is *Juliana Ng* aced the exam and very kindly let me copy her answers.

Praise be to you Juliana Ng wherever you are, that was extremely decent of you and it certainly taught me a lesson. A really boring one about how cheats never prosper. That was drilled into me as a kid, and I was so conscious of never cheating because I really feared never prospering. But then at age fifteen, after a lifetime of responsible behaviour, I thought maybe this prospering business was overrated?

So I cheated and I got my exam paper back with a big red 98% in a circle at the top of it! And all I could think was, *Well, well, well, looks like this cheat is prospering it up big time!*

Oh, and so as not to besmirch Juliana Ng's perfect maths record, I need to point out that she did not get 98 per cent on her exam, she got 100 per cent. She was a maths genius, I was just very canny about my cheating and intentionally got one question wrong so as not to 'trigger suspicion'. I know. Teenagers are so clever.

Anyway, turns out, tediously, that the old saying was right and my prospering was short-lived. My cheating propelled me into the top maths class where I couldn't keep up at all. I had not a clue what was going on. This was not helped by the fact that we had a totally unqualified nun teaching our class, who knew even less than I did. Her way of teaching calculus was to say, 'Girrrrrls, let us all bow our heads and pray. We ask thee, our lord and saviour, Jesus Christ, for some divine guidance today as we tackle sin, cos, and tan.'

My guess is this nun was assigned to the top maths class because these were the students (with one exception, obviously) who didn't really need teaching. They all just 'got' maths and could work straight from a textbook with no assistance. Unfortunately, I needed assistance and I needed it from someone a little more hands on than our lord and saviour Jesus Christ.

I don't imagine many schools still have nuns. These days nuns are like pandas, they're an endangered species, they're black and white and the numbers are dwindling because it's notoriously hard to get them to breed.

By the end of year eleven I'd fallen so far behind I was forced to drop maths altogether, there was no way I could have continued on to year twelve.

People were appalled that I would drop maths. I think the school even had to make a few phone calls to find out whether it was actually legal. I was quite the pioneer when it came to not doing stuff.

I was actually okay at maths until about fifth class. I realise that's not saying much because up until then it's pretty much just adding, subtracting, dividing and timesing, or 'multiplying' if you prefer to use fancy maths words. But I was good at all those things. I could even do fractions. Decimals hurt my head a bit but I managed. Then in fifth class they introduced letters into maths and that's when it all got really confusing. What were 'x' and 'y' doing in maths? It's very easy to feel stupid when you struggle with maths, which I think is why a lot of kids choose to mentally bail out and start excusing their poor marks by saying, 'I'm just not a maths person.'

It doesn't help that there are still a lot of teachers who explain maths like this: 'What do you mean you don't get it? There's nothing to get, it just is!' Then they stab repeatedly at a number they've written on the board or underline something multiple times and expect you to say, 'Ahhhh. I see! I didn't understand until you shouted at me and did a bunch of aggressive stabbing and underlining but now, all perfectly clear, let's move on.'

Fortunately I had a great teacher in fifth class, one of the best. Hats off to you, Mrs Craig, wherever you are! Mrs Craig didn't yell at me or make me feel stupid when my maths wheels started to fall off.

One day she was trying to explain the finer points of what 'x' represented and how it wasn't always the same in every equation—which was a concept I just couldn't grasp. I started to get upset and the more Mrs Craig tried to explain it, the more upset I got, to the point where I began to cry. (Crying because I couldn't do maths? Wow, what a zoob.)

Mrs Craig didn't get angry, she simply said, 'Hey, hey, hey, it's only maths, we cannot have tears because of maths.' She then picked up my book and threw it out the window. And sure, throwing the book out the window didn't exactly help me understand algebra but it did make me stop fretting about being an idiot. And it was pretty funny. That's what was most impressive about it, the fact that she knew humour was the thing most likely to motivate me.

I was so lucky not to end up in the other fifth-grade class. Their teacher was the yin to Mrs Craig's yang. In two whole years I never saw this woman crack a smile once. And because I intend to paint her as miserable and humourless, I won't use her real name, instead I'll call her Miss Snapsalot. No I won't, that sounds too much like a character from an Enid Blyton book—some cranky old bat who wants to chop down the magic faraway tree because it's full of golliwogs and gays or something. So I'll just call her Miss Holler. Which is fitting because as well as being permanently grumpy, Miss Holler was a yeller. That was her key motivational tool. Yelling. She was like Al Pacino in every single movie he's ever been in—what an annoying yeller that man is. Miss Holler was the same, always with the yelling. And even though she wasn't my teacher, I had to endure her yelling on a daily basis because she took the entire fifth grade for recorder 'training'—not practice, training.

Just as football is the religion at some high schools in America, recorder was the religion at my primary school. Unlike American high schools, however, where only the athletically gifted kids have to play football, every student at our school—whether musically ept or inept—was forced to play the recorder. So each morning at 9 a.m. when the bell rang, instead of going to our normal classes, we went straight to the hall for half an hour of recorder training with Miss Holler. Half an hour. Every single morning. For two years of my life. And to what end? Exactly how am I supposed to use these recorder-playing skills of mine? The only people I've ever seen make cash money out of playing the recorder are those ubiquitous Bolivian buskers who pop up in every pedestrian mall in every city in the world. Maybe I could brush up on my recorder skills, put my hair in plaits, whack on a poncho and see if they've got a gig going, they do seem to be touring endlessly.

I can also play a mean ruler. That's because if you forgot your recorder, you had to play your ruler. That's not a joke. You held your ruler to your mouth and sat there with everyone else and 'played' along, in silence (obviously), practising your 'fingering' on your ruler. Fingering. (Heh heh, can't believe how many times Miss Holler said fingering and she never found it funny once.) Parents, I'd encourage your kids to learn the ruler, it's certainly a lot more pleasant to listen to than the recorder.

Miss Holler never found anything funny. Mind you, she did have a pretty huge workload, which may be the reason she was always in a foul mood. She had her own fifth class, 5H, to teach, plus she taught recorder and ruler, and on top of that she was also the choir mistress. As if all that wasn't enough, she also 'trained' the much-lauded (by Miss Holler) school madrigal group. Choir was compulsory for everyone but the madrigal group was only for a select group of talented students, all of whom were handpicked by Miss Holler.

The madrigal group practised before and after school and, lucky them, they got to sing original songs which, I believe, were often penned by Miss Holler herself. One year, the songs were all about colours.

I remember one that went:

Red flaming firey!
Red flaming firey!
Scorching, scorching, scorching!

I think that one was about red.

There was another that went:

Green Green
The colour of trees . . .

And there was yet another about the enigma that is grey, which went:

Grey as a mouse
In a tumbledown house.

It was good stuff.

To be fair, you need to imagine those lyrics sung in four- and five-part harmony. That was the real beauty of the madrigal group—the harmonies. When you sing 'Greeeeeen Greeeeeen the colour of treeeheeeheeees!' in five-part harmony, it doesn't sound nearly as prosaic as it does when you read it on a page.

It goes without saying, I wasn't selected for the madrigal group. I didn't really mind, it gave me more time to focus on my ruler playing, which was really coming along a treat. I did, however, still get to perform with the Madrigals one year at the combined school choirs concert held at Willoughby Town Hall. On that incredibly auspicious occasion, I was tasked with the important job of being a live prop or set decoration. When the madrigal group took the stage to sing their repertoire of originals, this time themed around *Alice in Wonderland*, someone (I'm betting not Miss Holler) had the idea of adding a bit of colour and movement to the stage with some real-life *Alice in Wonderland* characters. Alice, the White Rabbit, the Red Queen etc. Basically, these characters would waft around the stage helping parents work out what the theme was, in case it wasn't clear from the (not particularly obtuse) lyrics.

Alice! Alice! Alice in Wonderlaaaand!
White Rabbit Whyyyyyy-te!
White Rabbit Whyyyyyy-te!

Again, it's important to imagine it sung in five-part harmony and with a really crisp 'T' sound on the end of whyyyyyy-*te*. And you also need to imagine Miss Holler out on stage conduct-ing so you understand how incredibly seriously she took it. She had all the conductor moves. She'd point at different sections with one hand to bring in a harmony while keeping tempo with the other hand. She did the traditional slow raising of the upwards-facing palm to build them to a crescendo and, of course, the favourite of every conductor, the slow circular open hand movement that then *snaps* to a close and brings the choir to a neat and complete stop. This particular night was her Carnegie Hall moment.

I had been anointed (by Mrs Craig) to play the Whyyyyyy-te Rabbit and I was delighted because as the White Rabbit, I not only got a rabbit outfit, I also got a blue velour waistcoat with gold buttons, handmade and sewn from a pattern by my long-suffering mother. Velour. My god, I loved that fabric more than Viyella. It was like velvet, only softer. I imagine if God had a vagina it would be made of velour. (I have included that sentence to fulfil my obligation as a female comedian to have a bit of celebratory vagina talk in my book.)

I don't remember much of what we were supposed to do on stage, probably because we weren't actually supposed to do much. At one point while the madrigal group sang, I was supposed to sit quietly on the big *Alice in Wonderland* chair and do nothing. Whoever thought that was a good idea was an idiot. I was ten years old. Do you really think you can ask a ten-year-old in a rabbit suit and a fabulous blue velour waistcoat to sit still on a stage for ten minutes? To ask them to do absolutely nothing while a bunch of kids warble out a bunch of songs about the Jaberwock-wock-wock-wockeeeeeey and Cheshire Cheshire Cheshire Catssssssss-ahhhhh?

A minute or so into the singing, I decided it would be really funny if I pretended to fall asleep and start snoring. Clearly quite a few parents thought it was funny too. Hearing the laughter only encouraged me and I started sliding off the chair and waking up with a start when I hit the floor. I tried to block out the music by putting a finger in one ear and my carrot in the other. I then took a bite of the carrot but had to spit it out cos it tasted of ear wax. Hilarious stuff. What was truly hilarious, though, was the fact that I thought I would be hailed a hero for my fantastic work. I secretly wondered if I might get some sort of prize at the next school assembly. I wasn't sure what kind of prize exactly, because this was before schools invented the idea of just handing out made-up prizes to everyone.

Afterwards, backstage, I saw Miss Holler stalking up and down the corridors obviously looking for something. A white rabbit it turned out. She spotted me and shouted, 'You! Stay right where you are!' while steaming towards me. Any thought that she might be coming over to thank me for my terrific animations on stage vanished. I turned tail and ran into an empty dressing room, which was a mistake. She followed me in there and now we were out of sight, with no witnesses. I half expected her to pull out a sock with a pool ball in it and start swinging it at me. She was so angry, I think she genuinely hated me. And who could blame her?

There was a lot of yelling about how I'd ruined the evening with my selfish, focus-pulling antics. I didn't quite understand what 'focus-pulling antics' meant. Fortunately, my dad explained it to me in the car on the way home, along with a few other words such as 'upstaging' and 'hamming it up'. Apparently I'd not only been an upstager but a ham as well. Christ, what a disaster . . . and yet, I don't want to go on about it but the audience had really seemed to like it.

To be fair, Miss Holler had a point. The madrigal group had been practising all year for that concert and it was extremely poor behaviour on my part to pull focus. It was their time to shine. I understand now that upstaging other performers is a real no-no. (Not that there aren't performers notorious for upstaging. Alls I'm saying is that if you do it too often, you will not be very popular with your peers.) And the only thing worse than upstaging someone is upstaging them by inferring that their own performance is boring everyone to death. So on my very first attempt at upstaging, I'd hit the jackpot. At the time, I genuinely thought I was helping. In my mind, I was bringing this performance home and surely they'd all be grateful that I had been there to save the day. The way I saw it, up until I started putting in with my rabbity comic stylings, that madrigal group was really stinking up the room. I believe this shows that even at a young age, I could 'read the room'. It's a very valuable skill, especially if you go on to become a stand-up comedian. You need to be able to sense when you are losing an audience so you can change it up, or maybe pace it up or just *get off* if there's no way to win them back. Miss Holler might have been a dedicated teacher and musician but she couldn't read a room to save herself. She was like one of those cocky, second-rate comedians who seriously have no idea when the audience is bored senseless and barely tolerating them. Those comics who come off after every gig and say, 'Oh my god, I killed it out there!' and you think, *Wow, I just watched your entire spot and you died a death, what is wrong with your ears? Couldn't you hear them not laughing?*

The next day, Miss Holler had another crack at me in the playground, which was enough to send me scurrying off to the bubbler shed where my own teacher, Mrs Craig, found me crying. Again with the crying. Jesus, was there ever a time

I wasn't crying at school? I told her Miss Holler had yelled at me and she said Miss Holler had good reason to be angry. Then she quietly confessed that she thought what I had done was very funny—not right, but very funny. She also said I was not allowed to tell anyone she'd said that. I never did. And I don't think I ever said thank you either. So thank you, Mrs Craig, because of you I can't read a calculus table but I can read an audience. And somehow you knew, even back then, what was going to be far more important to me.

THE WISHBONE CHICKEN SHOP

As a kid I collected stamps, but I'm pretty sure I only did it because I thought having a hobby was compulsory. People were always asking me, 'What are your hobbies?'

The first time it happened, I went to my dad and asked, 'What's a hobby?'

He said, 'It's something like stamp collecting or coin collecting.'

'Like tennis?' I asked.

No, Dad explained. Tennis was a sport, not a hobby.

'Like playing jacks?' I asked. Not really. 'Reading?' That was more of a pastime.

Geez, I thought, no wonder people were obsessed with asking about your hobbies! They were elusive little suckers.

I was determined to find a hobby I liked because, I'll be honest, having a pile of used stamps wasn't really doing it for me.

I checked in with my dad again, regarding the definition of a hobby.

'Something relaxing that you like doing in your spare time,' he explained.

I thought about what I liked doing. 'Cooking?'

'Yes,' according to Dad, 'cooking could be considered a hobby.'

'Licking the spoon?' No, not a hobby. 'Collecting pigs?' Big double tick on that one. Apparently, any kind of collecting is usually considered a hobby. (Unless it's used underpants, then it's a fetish. Or the skin of your victims, then it's a crime.) Perfect, now I had an answer to the 'what are your hobbies' question. Cooking and collecting pigs.

My love of cooking goes back to my childhood. I would sit at the kitchen bench and watch in amazement as my grandmother made pasta. At this point I'd ask that you divest yourself of any images involving clouds of flour and a little old Italian nonna pounding away at a lump of pasta dough. There was none of that. My very un-Italian grandma had her own unique pasta recipe that involved pouring a jar of Chicken Tonight sauce (creamy mushroom flavour) over some precooked spaghetti, then popping the lot in the microwave. Her cooking genius was to co-opt a sauce designed for chicken and use it for pasta instead, no chicken required. That's canny cooking. She also whipped up 'authentic' Asian dishes with jars of KanTong (sweet and sour flavour usually, and on one occasion black bean, although that was deemed a little too foreign-tasting).

What I'm saying is I don't have the sort of wistful food memories that usually end up in a book.

I always knew the season was a-changin' when Nonna would open a window and the smell of fresh basil from her kitchen garden would come wafting in on the warm breeze. Summer was here at last!

Sometimes Poppa would disappear out back and return with a large hunk of hard, pale-yellow sunshine, hewn from the enormous wheel of imported Parmigiano he kept in the shed where it would age and become more delicious with every day. He'd break each of us off a small piece and we would close our eyes and relish the strong flavour, allowing the pungent perfectly ripened cheese to nourish our young souls . . .

My food memories of Grandma are less quixotic. She liked that powdery 'parmesan cheese' that came in a green can. I never really knew where that stuff came from until recently when I saw an infomercial for an invention called a Ped Egg—which is really just a cheese grater for your feet. I watched the lady demonstrate it, using the grater side to shave her feet, with the shavings collecting neatly in the attached egg-shaped container. When she tipped the foot shavings out into her hand, I thought, *Ahhhh, that's the stuff we used to put on our pasta, I always thought it smelled like feet!*

I have no wish to denigrate my grandmother. Far from it. Everything is about context and I see her as a fine example of a woman who enthusiastically embraced all the advantages of the modern world. Standard lunch fare was white bread 'cheese' sandwiches made with Kraft Singles. For Grandma, it was all about convenience and the convenience of the Kraft Single was unbelievable. You had cheese, already sliced, and then individually wrapped, in plastic, for freshness! Could the modern world get any better?

For all her love of convenience, Grandma still loved a bit of tradition—and Sunday lunch was that tradition. Every Sunday at her house there would be a proper baked dinner. Always a roast chicken. That was her signature dish. No microwaves, no pre-packaged sauces. Grandma's roast chickens were amazing—beautiful crispy skin and so tasty! No one could roast a chicken like Grandma could, in fact my own mother never even bothered trying. Why would she? She knew it would never be as good as Grandma's. To this day, my mother still does not cook roast chicken. Lamb yes, beef sure, chicken never.

I only discovered Grandma's dirty roast chicken secret years later. Every Sunday morning, she used to pop down the road and buy a barbecue chicken from the sadly-now-defunct Wishbone Chicken Shop in Manly. Then she'd put it on a platter, surround it with baked veggies (which she *had* cooked herself) and serve it up as if the whole lot had come straight out of the oven. There was no trickery involved, she wasn't trying to fool us and pass it off as her own home cooking, I just never thought to ask. Had I done so, she'd have told me straight out that she bought it.

Grandma's attitude was: Why waste all that time cooking something that the Wishbone Chicken Shop could do much better? It's a good point.

And who would ever begrudge a woman of her era for embracing every modern convenience. She lived through a time when something as simple as doing the laundry could take an entire day. When you had to cook three meals a day every single day. There was no such thing as take away or Uber Eats. Either you cooked a meal or the family didn't eat. And you probably had to go to the shops (shops plural—because everything was sold separately back then) if not every day, then at least several times a week because food used to go off. Remember how food used to go off? I find it a bit odd the way bread never goes mouldy anymore. And milk lasts a suspiciously long time too.

My grandmother saw those jars of everlasting, ready-made sauces, the plastic-wrapped slices of never-moulding cheese and packets of soup where you just added hot water as gifts handed down from God Almighty herself. Such things gave a woman her life back.

However, from a selfish point of view, it meant I wasn't going to learn to cook from my grandmother. I wasn't too concerned though, because I'd heard that when you went to high school, you could actually do a subject called home economics, which by all accounts meant cooking. How great was high school going to be? Cooking lessons? That had to be more fun than maths or science or recorder or ruler playing or any other subject. I couldn't wait.

What a massive disappointment my first day at high school turned out to be. Not to mention a huge reality check. My year was made up of one hundred and fifty (!) twelve- and thirteen-year-old *women*. One hundred and fifty, just in my year! There hadn't been that many kids in my entire primary school. And at primary school it was all kids. Now I was surrounded by women, every one of whom seemed to have spent the summer holidays focused on doing nothing else but pushing out breasts and growing pubic hair. I had never seen anything like it in my life. I still looked more like an eight-year-old. And in case you think I'm exaggerating, later on in the year, when one of the parents saw me marching down the catwalk in the year seven fashion parade, she put her hand over her mouth and said, 'Oowah, what's wrong with that little girl, is she retarded?'

I wasn't. However, in her defence, I *was* walking fairly erratically. I'd made a tennis skirt in textile and design class and had brought in my own tennis racquet as a prop to use on the catwalk. I came down the runway swinging away, keen to show people I really could play tennis, so no doubt I was also wearing my concentration face. My concentration face consists of a furrowed brow and no lips. When I concentrate I pull my lips back in over my teeth so there is just a hard, lipless line where my mouth should be. My entire family has the same concentration face. Except my mum. She's so relaxed. Or maybe she just never concentrates? Point is, when you combined my tiny frame with my large head of hair, my concentration face and the fact that I was swinging a racquet quite wildly, all while trying to walk jauntily in time to music, I don't really blame that woman for thinking our school had a very progressive enrolment purview and was pioneering the now far more common practice of letting the special needs kids learn with the 'normal' kids.

But what truly disappointed me on day one of high school, even more than my lack of bosoms (a disappointment I would continue to harbour until year eleven) was the fact that Monte Sant' Angelo Mercy College for Young Ladies had chosen to get rid of the home economics department. It was suddenly deemed sexist to teach girls to cook. I disagree with this entirely. Cooking should be taught as a matter of course to all students—male, female, gay, straight, trans. Everyone should learn to cook, it is a fundamental part of life and something you will use far more often than most of the other things you learn at school. I couldn't believe cooking was no longer an option. This was the 'Girls can do anything' era. That phrase appeared on the sides of buses, on billboards, everywhere. Girls in overalls, holding drills in the air! 'Girls can do anything!' Good message. Although at my school, the message was Girls can do anything, except cook.

I went home from school very upset (knowing me, I probably cried about it) and told my mum, who went to work on the problem immediately.

I sometimes think my mum missed her calling. She would have been a great fixer. If it wasn't for her pesky, scrupulous honesty, her impeccable morals and principles, she could really have made a name for herself in the underworld working for the mob as a *Pulp Fiction*-style fixer/cleaner.

Mum called her sister, Judy, and arranged for her to give me a weekly cooking lesson. Judy was the real deal, a great cook, a former home economics teacher at TAFE *and* a major contributor to *The Macquarie Dictionary of Cookery*, which is an excellent reference book that still sits on my shelf today, I highly recommend it.

So every Monday I would take the bus to Judy's place after school for my cooking class. And that's how I learned to cook, from a practical, no-nonsense, home economics skilled auntie who took me through all the basics, from things like sautéing onions gently to bring out the sweetness, to learning what 'emulsification' means, to explaining why you should fold in egg whites with a metal spoon. Lesson one was pikelets, pancakes and scones and we progressed from there, eventually moving up to much grander fare like Beef Wellington and Duck à l'Orange. Don't judge. It was the eighties.

Auntie Ju taught me to cook with ingredients, measuring cups and attention to detail. She never once mentioned that I needed to cook 'with love'. Butter yes, lots of that. And salt, that was good too. But love? Meh. I think that whole cooking with your heart thing is overrated, you can't beat a recipe, a bit of know-how and good ingredients. Certainly no one has ever eaten something I cooked for them and said, 'Hmm, it was okay, just needed a bit more love.'

SCHNITZEL AND CHIPS

I would cook a lot more often but I simply don't have the time. I should clarify, I have plenty of time to cook. I just don't have the time to clean up the mess I make when I cook. It's unholy and quite often the state of my kitchen shocks even me.

If I am having a dinner party, I have to cook things that can be prepared well in advance in order to leave myself plenty of time to clean up, hose down and return the kitchen to an acceptable state. Something like lasagne is great. Lasagne can be prepared well ahead and then popped in the oven when guests arrive. The double-edged sword with lasagne is that there are two sauces and several pots required, which means it ranks really highly on the unholy mess scale. So while my lasagne is delicious, it does come at a price. The kitchen looks

51

like a bunch of bears have broken in, completely trashed the joint—and then very kindly left me a lasagne by way of apology.

I'm pretty sure there are men who have left me because they got tired of cleaning up the amount of mess I made in the kitchen when I cooked. Because the rule I grew up with and maintain still is that 'One person cooks, the other cleans up.' Mind you, if memory serves, I'm pretty sure that only *became* the rule after my dad started doing some of the cooking. Before that, I don't recall Mum cooking us schnitzel, chips and salad and then Dad coming in afterwards, clapping his hands efficiently and saying, 'Alrighty you lot, out of the kitchen while I deal with this mess your mother has made!' Then again, that could be because there was never any mess. My mum is from that generation of women who came out of the womb knowing how to clean as they go. It wouldn't surprise me to learn that my mother snipped her own umbilical cord, wound it up and pressed it into the doctor's hand, saying, 'Pop that in the bin for me would you please?'

Mum hated frying, not for health reasons but because of the mess. That's why she would only make schnitzel and chips once a year, on my birthday. In our house, the only time we ever got asked the question 'What would you like for dinner?' was on your birthday. Unfortunately for my mother, every year I would choose schnitzel and chips. My sister always chose something lame that involved broccoli. She genuinely loves vegetables, so much so that I reckon she'd even have eaten that yoga camp slop at Mangrove Mountain. A side note here for any parent who worries because their child is a picky eater or doesn't eat vegetables: stop worrying. My sister had a hearty appetite, always ate whatever was put in front of her, including all her greens, and yet she was a pale and sickly child, always wheezing and getting days off school because her lung had collapsed or something else just as attention seeking. I'm pretty sure if we'd lived in Victorian times, she actually wouldn't have made it past nine, the consumption would have taken her. Or rickets. Or some other Dickensian disease. Meanwhile, all I ate was meat and potatoes, my only concession to vegetables being a raw carrot that Mum would plonk on the side of my plate every night. I swear I didn't touch broccoli until I was thirty, mushrooms until I was thirty-three and cauliflower only fairly recently. I still won't eat peas (those things are mealy little balls of fart-flavoured paste if you ask me) yet I never missed a day of school. My mum thought it wasn't fair that I never got to have a day off school so at the end of every year she would let me take a 'sick day' and we would go to the cafeteria at the now defunct Grace Brothers department store at Warringah Mall and toast my good health with my two favourite food groups, a chocolate milkshake and a whole bowl of crinkle cut hot chips.

These days, on my birthday, Mum and Dad like to take me out for dinner to a fancy restaurant of my choice. Fortunately for them, the famed Grace Bros cafeteria is long gone otherwise I'd probably choose to go there. I think I might request a bit of retro dining for my next birthday and suggest that we stay in so Mum can fry up a storm and make me schnitzel and chips (no need for the salad). And as a special birthday treat, I'd like to see Dad clean up the kitchen afterwards.

THE GREAT WIFE SWAP

At age eleven I was convinced my parents were about to get divorced. This was despite the fact that they had never had so much as a cross word in front of me. I'm not saying they never had arguments, I'm sure they did, they just never had them in front of me. Emotional conservatism was our family cornerstone. You'd never guess at our Irish Catholic ancestry, there was no screaming, no dramatics and no wild drunken antics. Essentially, we were Irish Catholics doing an excellent impression of uptight, puritanical Protestants.

The reason I thought a divorce was imminent was because, at the time, everyone around us was doing it. Couples were dropping like flies, so I thought for sure my parents would be next and I was determined to make sure it didn't happen.

I am the eldest child—ergo I am a control freak. I'm told it's quite unusual for an eldest child to be a comedian, stand-ups are more likely to be the baby of the family because the youngest is usually the one who takes the most risks and doesn't worry about the consequences. By contrast, eldest children are born worriers. Probably because when you are the first-born, the world as you know it comes to an abrupt end when your sibling arrives (uninvited) on to the scene. Suddenly you realise nothing will ever be the same again. And not only that, the status quo can never be trusted, it's changed once, it could change again, so you worry constantly about what *might* happen, what else *could* upset your fragile world. For the record, my world was only made better by the birth of my sister. Eventually.

In the beginning, however, when she was a baby, she was just a bit of a slug who didn't do much and I couldn't really see the appeal. In fact, I'm not sure I even knew her name was Penny until she was about two. Up until then, I thought her name was either 'Careful!' or 'Gently!' or 'Mind Her Fontanelle!' Honestly, the fact that humans are born with soft, unclosed skulls surely signifies that we are not yet fully evolved. Newborn giraffes, horses, cows are all up and about walking in minutes whereas humans? We're born with a hole in our heads like some kind of human-hybrid-dolphin creature. It's a miracle we've remained at the top of the food chain for so long.

By the time I was eleven, Penny's skull had hardened and I'd really come around to the whole sister thing. I had a brother by then as well, although he was still in the fairly useless soft-skull slug stage. Penny, on the other hand, was now my very own genuine sidekick—she went along with everything. And that's the unique selling point of a younger sibling right there. Parents should stop trying to hype up the excitement of a 'new brother or sister to play with' and instead tell the existing child that the thing growing in mummy's tummy will be their very own butler/personal manservant. Because it takes younger kids forever to wise up to the fact that they don't actually have to do whatever the older kid tells them. Idiots.

Anyway, I took my trusty, unpaid idiot/assistant aside and shared my concerns with her about Mum and Dad's pending divorce. Clearly it had never crossed Penny's mind and she got a little panicky. I quickly reassured her it was all fine, I had a plan and would take care of it. All she had to do was back me up and stick to the plan. When Mum and Dad announced they were getting divorced (which would be any day) we would conduct a Norma Rae, stop-work type of walkout. (I was a huge Sally Field fan, I watched *The Flying Nun*, *Cannonball Run*, anything she was in, including the slightly age-inappropriate film *Norma Rae* about union busting and poor working conditions in factories. What I remember vividly about that film was that Sally took a stand on tables long before any of those *Dead Poet Society* wannabes.) Our divorce protest would take the form of refusing to live with either Mum or Dad and instead going to live with Grandma. Grandma had not been consulted about this but I was pretty sure she liked us so I was confident she'd go along with it.

Penny wasn't convinced about the plan to up sticks and move to Grandma's house. (To be honest, I think she was just worried about whether she'd be allowed to take her Barbies or not. Mum was canny and Penny obviously suspected she might use them as a bargaining chip. 'Alright, you can go but the Barbies stay here. So what'll it be? Grandma's House or the House with Barbies?'

No question Penny would have caved and chosen the House of Barbies. She loved those things more than I loved sugar.

My brother was not a factor in proceedings as he was too young to be included in the protest. At two years old, we were never going to be able to keep him on our side of the picket line. He was still at that awkward age where any dissent is managed by the parent tucking you under one arm, turning you into a human football and marching off with you even if you're flailing around in protest. So I knew he'd never be able to hold his ground.

After waiting and waiting for what seemed like an eternity for my perfectly happy parents to drop their divorce bomb, I thought a pre-emptive strike might be best so I went to my mother and laid out our terms. I told her that if she and Dad ever got divorced they could say goodbye to their kids (except the human football, obviously, they could keep him by default) but Penny and I would be leaving to live with Grandma.

Mum wasn't exactly threatened by my ultimatum, if anything she was mildly amused and slightly intrigued about what might have sparked it. She seemed totally oblivious to the fact that three couples who were good family friends of ours, all with kids we *used* to hang out with, had just separated. Not to mention the recent spate of swinging that had engulfed our boring suburban neighbourhood and resulted in an incredibly bizarre wife-swapping incident.

I don't know how it started, in fact, I will never understand how wife-swapping starts. Not from a moral standpoint but because I can't get my head around the logistics. Who suggests it and when? What signs do you look for that tell you a couple would be up for a bit of 'I'll show you my wife if you show me yours'. At what point during dinner with the Petersons does someone casually moot how fun it would be to fuck each other's wives?

By all accounts there was a fair bit of 'swinging' and 'swapping' going on in our remarkably average neighbourhood. I'm reliably informed that Catholics were never invited to 'those type' of parties, which meant my parents were exempt. How amusing that the Catholics were regarded as pillars of virtue. These days if you were up for engaging in a bit of morally reprehensible behaviour the Catholics would probably be first to get the tap. Certainly the Catholic clergy anyway.

The year everyone was getting divorced coincided with the year of the most notorious neighbourhood wife swap in the history of ever. To this day I'm still not sure whether the party that set the swap in motion would be hailed as a huge success or a massive failure. I guess it depends on how you look at things. What happened at this party was a permanent swap.

That's right, they 'borrowed' the library book but they never returned it. Surely, that's not allowed? Aren't there rules at these parties which stipulate that while you're allowed to take the 'book' into a private room and 'read' it, you must return the 'book' to the shelf once you are done 'reading'? You're not allowed to take the 'book' home with you, put it on your own shelf and then 'read' it whenever you feel like it.

Well, that's exactly what these couples did.

Post-party, the wives packed their bags and swapped houses, husbands and eldest children. Each family had two boys and the wives took their youngest boy with them to live in the new house with the new husband and left the eldest child in their former house with their former husband, forming two brand-new blended families each consisting of a mummy, a daddy and two children who would no doubt spend a lot of their adult lives in therapy.

The element of the story that made the whole thing all too convenient was that they lived (and continued to live) directly opposite one another. And it was this particular detail that always led me to imagine the swap happening in a very neat, sanitised, fifties' American-sitcom way.

Open on a wide shot of Wife One, Lou-Anne, in the bedroom. She has a suitcase open on the bed and is moving back and forth, taking her clothes from the closet and placing them neatly in the case. Next she moves into the ensuite bathroom, packing her cold cream (*what is that stuff?*) and other toiletries into a small, hard makeup case. As she returns to the bedroom, we notice there is a ten-year-old boy, her eldest son, Dwayne, sitting on the bed watching.

'Momma?' he says, 'Why cann't I come witch you?'

(*I have no idea why they are Southern all of a sudden, it's just how I used to see it in my head.*)

'Oh Dwayne honey, one day you'll unnerstand. Till then you needa be my brave soldier, you needa stay here and look after yo daddy for me. Come on little man, no tears now, I ain't goin' far, I'm only goan be across the way. Lookit, I'll show yew.'

(*I realise they've now turned into hillbillies and I apologise, I can't explain it.*)

Wife One, Lou-Anne, and her first-born, Dwayne, move to the bedroom window and she points across at the house opposite.

That's when we realise that an identical scene has been playing out across the way. In the house opposite, Wife Two, Clara, is also standing in the bedroom window with her eldest son, Larry, pointing across at the house opposite.

Clara picks up the dialogue where Lou-Anne left off. It's seamless.

'. . . and that's where Momma's goan be and she's goan wave to yew eva night, so don't you fret now, evathin's goan be alright, yew'll see.'

Cut to a wide shot of the street. Both front doors swing open simultaneously. Wives One and Two, Lou-Anne and

Clara, exit their houses clutching a suitcase with one hand and a small boy with the other. These are the youngest sons. The chosen ones, the ones who will accompany Momma on her journey across the way to start a new life in a new house with a new daddy. The boys each carry their momma's makeup case. Momma's little helper. The women nod as they pass one another crossing the street, but do not break stride.

Cut to the bedroom window, where Dwayne sits, watching proceedings unfold in the street beneath him. The camera moves in slowly, his face fills the frame and we see a single tear run down his cheek. Slowly, he raises his hand and waves. Is he waving at his momma? His lost little brother? No. The camera swings around to show the house opposite and we see that he's waving at Larry. Larry is sitting in the bedroom window waving back at Dwayne. A single tear runs down his cheek. Life has dealt these boys a cruel blow. They now have to live with their arsehole dads, the same arsehole dads who thought it was a good idea to treat their wives like stolen library books.

FIN

That's honestly how I imagined it happening. And while I could easily imagine Mum and Dad getting divorced, I never entertained the thought that they would borrow any of our neighbours' 'library books'.

My parents never did get that divorce, I assume in large part thanks to me and my brilliant plan.

GRANDE DAME
AT THE DANCE

My dad's style of parenting runs counter to my mum's, which is probably what makes them the perfect pair. While Mum is a realist who's notoriously difficult to impress, Dad is completely blind to all my faults. And not just me, there's no favouritism, he also thinks my sister is incredible (to be fair, she *is* pretty amazing), and as for my brother, to hear Dad tell it, my brother is the second coming of Christ, only heaps better.

My brother is a cook, a very good one. I'd say he was a 'chef' but he never finished any formal training, although my dad would say that's because he didn't *need* formal training, he was a natural at whatever he turned his hand to. Which was kind of true. At sixteen, he grew a hell of a marijuana plant.

It was taller than a human man—and that was just the one we found. I'm sure there he had a whole plantation happening somewhere.

I can't resent Dad for his incredibly positive (and possibly a tad inflated) opinions of my siblings because his generosity of spirit also extends to me. Honestly, my dad thinks I pooh solid gold. This was never more evident than at my year ten formal.

In the sixties my grandmother made all my mum's formal frocks. Gran was a fantastic seamstress and my mother was an excellent clothes horse. With my mum's immaculate hairdos and her vogue, made-to-measure gowns, she'd have fit right in to any scene from *Mad Men*. I've seen the photos.

Unfortunately, I do not take after my mother. As mentioned previously, the Vardy Party was the last time I ever left the house looking 'on trend'. And that was largely because my mother put that ensemble together. Once I started taking charge of my own outfits, things really went downhill for me. I wasn't allowed to have my ears pierced but that didn't stop me from finding a fun, non-body-invasive way to accessorise. At around the age of nine, I started wearing brooches. Large, statement-making brooches. I think the statement I was making was, 'Hello world, I am nine going on sixty-seven!' Among my favourites were a silver penny-farthing bicycle, a pig face made of clay, and a colourfully painted parrot made of wood.

You wouldn't think it could get any worse than pinning slabs of timber and pottery on my tiny frontage but then in my teens I went completely off the rails and developed a penchant for grey corduroy and maroon velour. At a time when everyone else was wearing acid-wash denim jeans and hyper-colour fluoro T-shirts, I preferred to look like a spinstery maths teacher who will one day be jailed for stealing a baby out of a pram in a supermarket.

What I'm saying is I have never had any idea about fashion and I still don't, which is why, these days, I spend my life in jeans and a T-shirt. It's also the reason I prefer to wear a suit on television. I'm not making a statement with that look, I'm just trying to avoid making mistakes. By sticking to a suit, the only decision I have to make each week is which tie, which shirt? And even then, I usually consult with the wardrobe department, just to make sure.

In my teenage years, when I wasn't out painting the town grey in my corduroy knickerbockers (seriously), my safety outfit was tennis gear. I played a lot of tennis and the only place I really rocked it was on a tennis court. I would often put my tennis clothes on even when it was raining and I knew we wouldn't be playing because I didn't know what else to wear. When my mother inevitably questioned why I was dressed for tennis, I would look up at the sky ponderously and say, 'Looks like it could fine up.'

If only I could have worn a tennis dress to the year ten formal.

It was the eighties, which was a very sad time for teenage fashion. It was all taffeta, ruffles, puffy sleeves, bubble skirts and tube skirts. Quite rightly, I rejected all those things. Quite wrongly, I put together my own ensemble. Weeks before the dance, Mum took me to David Jones where I eschewed the racks of brightly coloured formal dresses made for girls my age and instead wandered off into women's wear. Not *young* women's wear but middle-aged women's wear—brands like Perri Cutten and Carla Zampatti—where I found myself admiring the well-cut clothes. I chose a sensible long skirt that finished a few inches above the ankle. I think my mother had to take it in about six inches because no doubt it was made for a mature woman who'd had several children and didn't have much of a waist anymore. But I thought it was perfect, I particularly liked the extra bit on the bottom of the skirt. It wasn't enough to make the skirt a fashionable fishtail but rather gave it just a hint of sensible middle-aged mermaid. Oh, and it was black—that's a fun colour!

A top proved harder to find but eventually I came across a shapeless, long-sleeved, watercolour silk top in a little boutique, the name of which escapes me but if I had to guess I'd say it was probably called 'Joanne's' or 'Lesleigh–B's' or 'Clothes for Old Women' or something. It was clearly a shop that specialised in grandmother-of-the-bride type outfits but I didn't spot that at the time. I was blinded by the muted turquoise and grey (my favourite!) sack of a blouse, which I thought would provide the perfect pop of colour when teamed with my classic black skirt. It was a thing of beauty, that blouse, with long billowing sleeves and high round neckline.

After I settled on the top—which hung off me like a bag—
my mother asked me just once, 'Are you sure that's what you
want?' I was and, credit to my mother, she bought it for me
without saying another word. I also wanted a 'really big' black
sash to pull everything together. Again, my mum said nothing,
she just bought the fabric and made me a giant sash.

The result was an outfit any woman would have been
thrilled to wear . . . if she was sixty and going to dinner at the
yacht club. Sadly, I was fifteen.

Sadder still, I genuinely thought I had nailed it, right up
until I saw the look of horror on my date's face. All the other girls
were dressed in acres of taffeta and lace, with huge, hairsprayed
quiffs at the front of their heads. My mum had blow-dried my
hair for me, and though it wasn't great, I was very happy with
it at the time. Looking back, I can see that it looked a lot like
a removable helmet of hair. It was seriously reminiscent of the
heavily lacquered wig Eric Bana would eventually wear on *Full
Frontal* when he impersonated Ray Martin. I was also sporting
a very grown up shade of 'raisin' lipstick that I'd borrowed from
Mum's makeup drawer. Raisin. My date was absolutely horrified at the appearance of this matronly 'grande dame'. It was
clear he wanted nothing to do with me, not just from his expression but also from the fact that he was later dragged out from
under the head table where he'd been busted pashing some
girl from another school. I don't blame him at all.

I've since had friends point out that the fifteen-year-old me
in my year ten formal photos looks a lot like Rhonda, the PR

woman character I play in the TV series *Utopia*. Only Rhonda looks a tad younger. And better dressed.

But that's not what my dad saw. He told me later that he couldn't believe how beautiful I looked. His genuine interpretation of the scene was that my date's eyes had 'lit up like he had just won the prize'. Those were his exact words.

My dad truly thought I looked stunning. Either that, or he is the most convincing actor of all time and he missed his true calling and he is the one who should have been on the stage. Either way, what a wonderful man.

PART TWO

HITCH-HIKING, OLDER MEN AND OTHER BAD DECISIONS

THE FANCY FIG

I left school not having a clue what I wanted to do with my life. My half-hearted showbiz ambitions had been crushed first by my parents, then by Miss Holler, and finally by a crippling case of teenage acne that meant I wasn't willing to show my face anywhere, let alone on a stage in front of an audience.

I had a stab at a few things, mostly things that other people told me I'd be good at. Like the communications degree at the University of Technology, which was purported to be a terrific course. I'm not sure exactly who purported that myth, and to be fair it probably was and is a good course, it just wasn't the experience I was looking for when I signed up for university straight out of school.

Pre-Frank Gehry's polarising 'brown paper bag' structure, the central UTS campus was just one brutalist high-rise building. That was it. A single tower block of about thirty-two floors. No beautiful 200-year-old sandstone buildings with gargoyles, no impressive architectural history, no covered walkways or cloisters, no quadrangles and, more importantly, no broad selection of bars and cafes catering to all types of students, from the bookish dag to the pretentious wannabe intellectual to the politically idealistic table thumper. Instead, there was an underground bunker that served as the cafeteria/bomb shelter. In other words, UTS had a real hide calling itself a university.

The diversity of courses offered at UTS was reflected in the student body. Civil engineering, electrical engineering, bio-medical engineering, environmental engineering, engineering, engineering, engineering. And communications. There were about a hundred of us doing the communications course in a sea of thousands of fun-loving engineers. Of those hundred communications students, 20 per cent were school leavers like me who'd got a decent mark and thought perhaps this course was a way to get into journalism. And that's what I thought I wanted to do. Maybe? I don't know. How can you possibly know what you want to do for the rest of your life when you're seven-teen? On the upside, everyone said it was a great course. (I'm very easily led by others.)

With the arrogance of youth, it seemed to me that the rest of the communications student body consisted of humour-less, mature-age students. Students who had, by the way, gone to great lengths to *earn* their place in the course. They had written submissions and done interviews to prove how much they wanted and deserved a place. They didn't just get a mark. These people had come to university to learn and study, they knew what they wanted to do with their lives, and they had a true vocation for the communications industry. Whatever that was. They were there to debate and participate intelligently in class discussions about the role of communications professionals in the public sphere. Whatever that meant. I turned up to lectures for about a week and participated by rolling my eyes at the 'dumbness' of it all. Such a formidable intellect. I really deserved my place there.

See, I didn't go to university to learn how 'public communication is practised in not-for-profit, for-profit and government sectors'. If I had, I'd probably be in some fabulous high-powered, high-paying job right now rather than traipsing around the country as a glorified clown/court jester. (For the record, I am not unhappy with the outcome.)

I went because I thought, or hoped, that university would offer me a social life, something which had been largely absent in my life thus far, unless you counted playing tennis on Saturday afternoons and then going up to the local bowling club afterwards for a glass of lemon squash with the team. My Saturday nights were mostly spent hanging out with my much younger brother watching *Eight is Enough* and *Magnum P.I.* Not that I didn't enjoy that—they were great shows and my brother was a very funny kid and excellent company.

So once it was clear the only social life on offer at UTS was the chance to hang out with engineers and talk about load-bearing walls or rehash the afternoon's tutorials over a glass of red wine with mature-age women (whose company I'd probably really enjoy *now*) I stopped going. Back then, the engineers didn't do it for me and I was still a ways off drinking wine and enjoying intelligent discussion. At that stage I was more into West Coast Coolers, Southern Comfort and Coke, and talking about my favourite episodes of *The Young Ones*.

After my exertions at UTS I enrolled at teachers' college. I imagined I was going to be a physical education teacher. To this day I could not tell you why I thought that was a good idea. Possibly I was lured by the prospect of a job that had fourteen weeks of paid holidays per year and didn't have all that time-consuming 'marking' teachers always go on about. Surely there was no marking in PE. All I'd be doing during my fourteen weeks of downtime would be shopping for tracksuits. That probably appealed to me as well, the fact that I wouldn't need to wear actual clothes to work. I could spend my life in sports gear.

After nine months in a tracksuit at teachers' college, I'd lost my passion for physical education. To be honest, I lost it a lot earlier than that but I was determined to stick it out to prove a point. My mother had laughed in my face when I told her I was going to become a PE teacher, just like she had all those years earlier when I told her I was going to 'get anorexia'. She threw her head back and said, 'Hah! PE teaching? This'll be good, I give it a month.'

Well I showed her, I gave it nine months. What a waste of everyone's time that was. God it's annoying when your mother is right.

While I was making my half-hearted efforts at university and college, I always had a part-time job at the Pizza Hut as a waitress. At one point it looked like that might be the only thing I would ever really excel at. I was a pretty good waitress, until I got cocky and tried to carry too many things at once and dropped a lava-like lasagne down a man's back. I know I should have felt bad about it, but seriously? Who orders lasagne at the Pizza Hut? The clue is in the title, it's not the Lasagne Palace, it's the Pizza Hut, just have a pizza. Also I've seen what's in those lasagnes. Trust me, just have a pizza. And maybe one of those white-iced gingerbread men that sit in a big glass jar at the register. You've probably always wondered, *Who the hell eats those?* Well, I did. In fact I bloody loved them. Pizza Petes they were called, soft stale gingerbread covered in rock-hard white icing, with a sparse covering of hundreds and thousands. Delicious.

Once I'd dropped out of teachers' college and given up on furthering my education, I had enough time on my hands to get a real job so I applied to be the receptionist at an optometrist's. I had grand plans. I was going to work there for a year and save up all my money to go overseas. I lasted one day. I don't think I have ever been more bored in my life. I wanted to poke my own eyes out with a stick, only it would have been pointless because the optometrist would have replaced my eyeballs free of charge and forced me to keep watching the clock in the shop, which I swear was moving backwards. There has never been a longer day than the one I spent working in the optometrist's. At the end of my 'trial day' they asked me how I'd enjoyed it and whether I'd like to take the job full-time. Tears filled my eyes and because my brain had shut down around lunchtime due to extreme tedium, I couldn't even manage to come up with a polite lie. Instead, I sobbed and told the optometrist I was so sorry but I couldn't possibly take the job because I would die of boredom. I literally thought I might die. (I need to remember this incident next time I'm being annoyed by a young person's histrionics. I, too, was once a melodramatic youth.)

Grand plans dashed, I went back to my one true calling, waitressing.

Thanks to my experience at the Pizza Hut, I had a (very short) CV and a reference (no one mentioned the lasagne incident), so I was able to apply for higher-end waitressing jobs. One of which was at a fancy restaurant called The Fig. I'm actually wondering now if perhaps it wasn't The Fig but The Prune . . . or The Grape. Whatever it was, it was definitely a fruit.

The Fig had advertised for day-shift waitresses and the

hourly rate was markedly higher than the minimum wage. I was still young and naïve enough to assume the reason they were paying so well was because they were upmarket, charged a lot of money and liked to pass on those profits to their wait staff in reward for their loyal service. Bless me.

It never occurred to me that a restaurant would pay more so that you would wear less. I still didn't twig, even after I'd spoken to the manager on the phone and he'd asked me if I was prepared to do the 'Businessmen's Lunch'. 'Sure!' I said, thinking *Why not? What's the big deal?* Businessmen have got to eat lunch, haven't they? And because I was very happy with the hourly rate I agreed to go in for the interview. Only then did I learn that 'Businessmen's Lunch' meant fat-arsed, soft-bellied, middle-aged men with no necks, in suits being served lunch by young women in lingerie. God almighty, where was the self-respect? And to be clear, I'm talking about the men in suits not the women in lingerie.

Sometimes I wonder how men have been the dominant sex for so long with the sort of brain that thinks it's a good idea to pay more money for average food because it's served by women in underpants. And aren't they embarrassed to admit that this is, apparently, the only way they get to see a real live woman in the almost-nude? Why not just be a decent, respectful human and then you might actually meet a woman who likes you enough to show you her underpants for free. Play your cards right and she might even cook you dinner, no extra charge. And to the restaurants that host these sorts of lunches, the same logic applies, just be better and serve quality food. If your food is any good you won't need to offer side orders of tits and arse.

I should have guessed what was going on as soon as I saw the hourly rate. And even during the interview I was still incredibly slow on the uptake. The penny only really dropped when the man interviewing me said my lingerie would need to be tasteful and that I would have to bring it in so he could approve it. Apparently diners at The Fig liked their waitresses to be classy not slutty. I do love it when morally bankrupt people get all righteous and principled. He also really sold the empowering nature of the job, telling me it was totally my choice whether I wanted to be 'a sitter' or not. Sitting was not compulsory, some of the girls just waitressed, no sitting. However, he added, I should bear in mind that 'sitters' often earned twice as many tips, and all you had to do for that extra cash was sit on a businessman's lap during dessert and spoon-feed him his chocolate mousse. 'Nothing slutty,' he reiterated. 'It's all tasteful and above board here.'

I turned it down, all of it, the sitting *and* the waitressing. Apart from anything else, I'm a real stickler for keeping my clothes on around food. There's something slightly unhygienic about having so many arseholes in such close proximity to food. And to be clear, once again, I'm talking about the men here not the women.

HOW AM I NOT DEAD?

My first boyfriend and I had been together for about a year when we decided to buy a pop-top VW Kombi van and drive it around Australia.

Delighted with our purchase, we drove it over to my parents' house and told them of our grand plan. I'm not sure Mum and Dad thought it was quite as brilliant an idea as we did, but fortunately there was a handy distraction present that day. Some friends of theirs had dropped over, along with some random German guy. I'm still not sure who he was, a friend of one of their friends perhaps.

When we announced to everyone that we were going to drive around Australia, the random German guy gave us two pieces of advice. The first was to buy a gun. We all laughed heartily—good one Random German Guy!—then we realised he was serious. He had travelled a lot, he said, and the one thing you always needed was a gun. He wasn't specific about what we would need a gun for, just that we would definitely need one.

I was thrilled, not because I love guns, but because all of a sudden the focus shifted from the inevitable debate about whether or not I should be driving around the country in a Kombi van, to why anyone would ever need 'a bloody gun'. That's what my dad kept calling it—'a bloody gun!' At one point it was 'a bloody gun, for Christ's sake!' Things started to get a little heated and I thought maybe Dad should back down. After all, Random German Guy probably had 'a bloody gun'. There was a bit of shouty back and forth about a gun being an essential travel tool and a bit of insult throwing as Dad came back with, *'You're* the bloody travel tool!' which is when Mum stepped in and shut the whole thing down with some of her trademark pooh-poohing.

She's a big pooh-pooher, my mother. She pooh-poohs a lot of things. Her favourite way to 'pooh-pooh' something is to make a scoffing noise and say, 'Don't be ridiculous.' And that's exactly what she said in the living room that afternoon.

'Alright, that's enough, no one is getting a gun. Pfff, you're all being ridiculous.' She then gave her signature, dismissive flick-of-the-hand gesture, as if waving away a pesky mosquito. And that was that. No more gun talk.

The second, far less controversial piece of advice Random German Guy dispensed was that we should pack a bar of ordinary Sunlight Soap. There was no objection to this from anyone, although we were all curious as to why we might need it. He explained, 'If you ever get a hole in your petrol tank you can mash up a bit of Sunlight Soap and use it to plug the hole.' Apparently some chemical reaction occurs between the soap and the petrol which causes the soap to set hard like cement, allowing you to keep driving until you can get the petrol tank fixed or replaced. He didn't say how you might come to have a hole in your petrol tank, but I assumed it would be from some trigger-happy, gun totin' German traveller taking pot shots at passing cars.

Armed with soap only, my boyfriend and I set off. We made it as far as Epping (about thirty minutes from home) before we had a major fight. Our plan had been to drive clockwise around the country, which meant heading south. We'd headed north. I blamed him. He blamed me. And I think it dawned on both of us right there in beautiful downtown Epping that this trip wasn't going to work out. But we turned around and drove on anyway. Clockwise this time.

We barely spoke for the next six weeks as we rumbled across the country. By the time we got to Perth, we found enough words to admit defeat and agreed to go our separate ways. He took the van and drove back to Sydney (probably via Epping) while I met up with other backpackers and travelled up the West Coast. Once I got to Broome, I decided the best way to continue my trip across the top end of Australia would be to hitchhike. By myself.

I have a theory about human brain development—it's that your fontanelle closes up shortly after birth but then reopens at some point in your late teens, allowing all the sensible out and all the stupidity in. It's the only explanation for why humans in their late teens and early twenties do such idiotic things. Things you look back on and go, 'Wow. How am I not dead?'

So with my fontanelle wide open and stupidity pouring in, I set myself up at a roadside truck stop just outside of Broome, intending to thumb my way across northern Australia. I wish I had a photo of me. I would caption it, 'What has two thumbs and an empty skull? This chick.'

As I stood waiting for a truckie or a traveller to pull up and offer me a ride, a guardian angel appeared in the form of a sensible grown-up woman who worked at the truck stop. To this day I still thank the fictional Baby Jesus that she was there. She asked me what I was doing and I told her of my simple, but awesome plan. To her credit, she very quickly saw the obvious flaw in my simple but awesome plan, namely that there was a very high probability I'd be raped, killed and dumped somewhere in the Never Never, never never to be found again.

I can totally see now that hitchhiking, on my own, was possibly the dumbest idea I've ever had—and I've had a lot of dumb ideas. But I was in my youthful immortal phase and saw myself as invincible, ergo, unrape-able and unmurderable.

In my mind, any truck driver who tried it on with me would be given a firm, 'No thank you, sir!' I might even give him a sharp bop on the nose if he got too persistent. That ought to do it. A firm no and a bop on the nose. Apparently, I thought sharks were doing a lot of the truck driving in the Top End.

Fortunately, the sensible grown-up woman at the truck stop had a far superior plan. She told me to come inside with her, sit down, have a cup of brown liquid (I think it was tea), and meanwhile she would vet potential rides for me. It didn't take long, just a couple of hours, before she'd selected a suitable transport and I was on my way across Australia in a station wagon with three lovely, posh English boys. I'm fairly sure she'd read them the riot act, warning them that she'd taken their names, descriptions and number plate and, should I go missing, she'd be calling the cops. Exactly what she said to them I don't know but those boys were absolute gentlemen and my trip turned out to be far more *Famous Five* than *Wolf Creek*. I earned my keep by sitting in the back of the station wagon making cheese and chutney sandwiches and passing them forward to the three jolly chaps up front. All that was missing were lashings of ginger beer, some delicious currant buns and Timmy the dog.

The lads and I were halfway across the Northern Territory when disaster struck. Only it wasn't a disaster, it was another gift from fictional Baby Jesus (I really need to start believing in that guy), this time in the form of a stone going through our petrol tank.

I don't think I've ever been happier. We were in the middle of nowhere, no service station in sight, the boys were panicking and I was about to be a hero. Turned out Random German Guy was right about the Sunlight Soap which, amazingly, I was still carrying around in my bag, right next to my gun. (I'm kidding. Of course there was no gun.) We plugged the hole and made it all the way to Queensland where we finally found a place to get the petrol tank replaced.

I was pretty sure I'd become some kind of urban legend among travellers—the tale of the twenty-something fool who cheated rape and death only to save the day by MacGyver-ing a petrol tank with an ordinary bar of Sunlight Soap.

But that would be missing the point. Because the real hero of this story was not Lady MacGyver and her Sunlight Soap but rather that wonderful woman from the truck stop outside Broome. We need to look out for our teens and twenty-somethings and we need to do it like this woman did, in a subtle and caring way. She didn't disparage me, she didn't call me a stupid idiot (not to my face anyway), she just ever so gently steered me away from certain death.*

---

* NB: I managed to make it all the way around Australia without ever needing a gun. In fact I've since travelled all over the world and not once have I found myself thinking, *Hmm, I could really use a gun right now!* So I'm not entirely sure what Random German Guy was on about. Maybe he liked to shoot his own food. Or hold up shops and steal his own food. Or kill people. Personally, I've found it quite easy to travel without ever doing any of those things.

EARN 1000 DOLLARS A WEEK, ASK ME HOW!

I'm old enough now to realise that there's always a catch when you're offered more money than usual to do a job. At twenty, however, I was still pretty dumb or, perhaps, full of hope is a nicer way to put it. So when someone turned up at the hostel I was staying at in Perth bragging about how you could earn a thousand dollars a week working at a crayfish factory in Geraldton, I jumped on a bus, travelled for seven hours, and applied in person the very next day. Two reasons. Firstly, that sounded like a tonne of money; and secondly, it definitely sounded like something you would do with your clothes on. I didn't know a lot about crayfish but I knew what they looked like and that no one in their right mind would want to handle those spiky, prehistoric lobstery things standing around topless or in lingerie. Although now I feel like I might have put the idea out into the universe and it won't be long before we see some kind of slasher porno film about women in a crayfish factory. My money is on it being called 'Attack of the Cock Lobster'.

Amazingly, you really could earn a thousand dollars a week working at a crayfish factory, and I was right about getting to do it fully clothed. There was of course a catch, which was that in order to earn the thousand dollars, you needed to work eighty hours a week rather than the standard forty because when crayfish season starts, the crayfish boats arrive chock-full of crays, and they need people working around the clock to process them. So the crayfish factory operated twenty-four hours per day and you worked till you fell over, went home for a couple of hours and then came back and started again.

My plan, grand as always, was to work there for the full twelve-week season and save up enough money to go overseas for a year.

I'm sure the full-time workers see the same thing every year when the cray season starts and the factory is forced to employ a bunch of itinerants to cope with the increased workload. No doubt it's very boring for the regulars. I imagine every year they get the same range of dumb hopefuls turning up expecting to make their fortune in a few weeks. Backpackers, students and disgraced Pizza Hut waitresses, none of whom have any idea what the job actually entails. They've just heard, 'Hey! You can earn a thousand bucks a week! Seriously! A thousand bucks!'

It wasn't difficult work, in that the tasks were fairly simple. However, it was physically demanding. You were on your feet for eighteen to twenty hours a day, it was a hot, smelly, sauna-like environment, and you needed to wear several pairs of rubber gloves to protect you from the boiling water and the crayfish spikes. The central area of the factory floor was occupied by an enormous rectangular bin that contained a giant steaming pile of freshly boiled crayfish, a pile that seemed to constantly regenerate itself like the Magic Pudding. My job was to take a crayfish from the pile, hose the crap off it (crayfish often crap themselves when they're thrown into boiling water, and who can blame them) then put it on the conveyor belt and watch it chug off to be sized, wrapped and boxed. The sizing, wrapping and boxing jobs were reserved for the permanent staff while the casuals like me got to be hosers. It was a messier, much wetter job and it was done standing up but the hardest bit of all, for me, was that you had to work in silence.

I'd only been there a few days and already the foreman had warned me, on several occasions, to just get on with the job and stop talking. And of course, instead of doing that, I told him that I was perfectly capable of hosing a crayfish *and* talking at the same time. 'This is not exactly brain surgery,' I said. Wow. What a dick. On so many levels. Firstly, that I said that to someone, but secondly, how dare I be so lame as to use a cliché like that. It's as bad as if I'd said, 'It's hardly rocket science.' The only saving grace is that I didn't say, 'It's hardly rocket surgery!' Always hilarious that one.

My punishment for talking back to the foreman was to be locked in the walk-in freezer for an hour. It was just like that *Brady Bunch* episode where Greg and Bobby got locked in Sam the butcher's cold storage room, except there was no tiny window for me to escape through. It was a pretty good punishment and I totally deserved it. Every twenty minutes or so the foreman would open the door and ask me if I was ready to come back to work, quietly. Twice I answered back, banging on about how it really was possible to work and talk at the same time. Twice the door got slammed in my face. By the third time, I was too cold to speak so I just nodded and went back to work, warming myself up over the mountain of steaming crayfish.

I stank even more than usual when I got home from work that day.

There is nothing quite like the smell of a crayfish factory. The good thing is, when you're at work, you only notice it for about the first ten minutes, after that the smell has permeated every part of you, your hair, your skin, your clothes, and you simply become part of the bigger stink. The problem is that having stood in that reeking miasma for eighteen hours, your nose is now deaf and you can't smell the crayfish stink on yourself anymore, however other people certainly can, which is why my flatmates refused to let me into the house whenever I came home and I had to stand in the yard while they hosed me down. The indignity of it. The hoser had become the hosed, to them I was just another crap-covered crayfish, or at least I smelled like one.

I'm sure if you tried to punish someone today by putting them in a walk-in freezer, there would be all sorts of repercussions. The foreman would definitely be called into HR and he would probably be fired for breaching dozens of rules regarding appropriate boss–employee conduct, not to mention the health and safety issues. The employee, on the other hand, would no doubt get some sort of counselling and six months off at full pay.

For the record, I got over my stint as a human popsicle without any counselling, and I do not have a fear of freezers— or crayfish for that matter. I actually think the foreman did the right thing. While it didn't get me to stop talking, it did get me to do it more quietly, which I'm sure everyone on the production line appreciated.

CATCHPHRASEY JOE

One of my favourite ways to break up with someone is to put distance between myself and my soon-to-be ex-partner. I have taken this method to extremes on occasion. I started by moving interstate and eventually graduated to moving countries and even hemispheres to end a relationship. Which leads me to believe that the 'distance method' of breaking up is a bit like taking ice (apparently) in that you need more and more each time in order for it to be effective.

My first of these 'It's not you, it's me . . . me not living in the same town as you ergo we cannot go out anymore' break-ups occurred when I was dating an older man. He was thirty-three. I was in my early twenties, back from my travels around Australia, and still wafting around aimlessly, unsure of what I was doing with my life.

I can see now that there was clearly something wrong with this man. Why else would he go out with a twenty-something part-time waitress, full-time university drop-out? Maybe he had control issues? Maybe he knew that dating a woman his own age would rob him of the opportunity to play the role of worldly-wise, elder statesman, guiding and shaping the young fawn. He certainly never tired of trotting out that patronising phrase, 'You will understand, one day, when you're older.'

At the time, I couldn't see that it was weird. I was young and, in *my* mind, I was fascinating, so why *wouldn't* this guy want to go out with me? Oftentimes this sort of May/September (or January/December, depending on how big the age gap is) relationship ends when the woman wakes up one day and realises she's perfectly capable of thinking her own thoughts, the first of which is usually, *Why on earth am I going out with an old man who keeps giving me earnest lectures about life?* Sure, it's fun for a while being introduced to olives and French Champagne and 'classic' films like *The Manchurian Candidate* and *An Affair to Remember,* but ultimately you're not a proper grown-up yet and given the choice, you'd be happier eating a packet of Twisties, watching *Pretty Woman* and supping on Midori & Lemonade. (Mmm. Sugar and green stuff. Sophisticated.) It's no real mystery what was in it for him. I was in the best shape of my life thanks to all the effort I put into doing absolutely nothing. That's right, I did nothing.

I left my makeup on when I went to bed. Ate crap food. Drank sugar in liquid form. Didn't go to the gym. Never drank any water, certainly not eight glasses a day. So what was my secret? Youth.

My advice to any young woman is to know that you are so hot right now. It's nature's trade-off for being not particularly interesting yet. You get to be awesome to look at. The mere fact that your skin is chock-full of collagen makes you beautiful. Older women try to buy that stuff in a jar, whereas your face is generating it 24 hours a day. So enjoy your rubbery body and your plump, beautiful, hydrated skin that no amount of money can buy, and don't waste a single minute worrying about your looks. You are hot.

The predictable way for this relationship to end would have been for me to come to my senses and say, 'Eww you're really old. See you later, Gramps!' or words to that effect. But that's not what happened. We broke up for a more unusual reason—we broke up because he used catchphrases and I think catchphrases belong in sitcoms from the seventies, eighties and, at a push, the early nineties. They do not belong in today's sitcoms and they have no place whatsoever in real life.

His most famous—and by famous, I mean tediously overused—catchphrase was the one he trotted out in response to, 'Hi, how are you?'

'I'm fine, mild and 27 degrees!' he'd say.

I often wondered what kind of reaction that got the first time he said it. Clearly it must have brought the house down otherwise why would he have deemed it worthy of another outing? And then another and another and another.

Every single time. 'How are you mate?' 'I'm fine, mild and 27 degrees!'

Pretty soon it became like nails down a chalkboard.

And in case you're thinking, *'That seems a bit harsh, it was only one catchphrase'*, let me assure you it wasn't his only one. He had plenty of others in his arsenal, he was a regular Steve Urkel. In fact I'm surprised people didn't stop and applaud every time he entered the room. (In his mind they probably did, and in fairness, I think he saw himself more as a Fonz than an Urkel.)

Some of his other classics included: 'Any better and they'd shoot me.'

But it's all about the delivery. He liked to draw out the 'a' in 'any', then run the rest together really quickly, then give it a long 'e' on the 'me'. So it went, 'Aaaaaaanybetteranthey'dshootmeee.'

We also never made it through the day without 'absotively' getting at least half a dozen outings. 'Want to go for a drink?'

'Absotively I do.'

And then there was: 'Don't go there!'

I think I hated that one even more than 'Fine, mild and 27 degrees!'

'Don't go there' is a favourite of second-rate breakfast radio crews. I'm talking about shows like, 'Bricko, Muggsy and Sue in the mornings!' You're never sure which one is Bricko or Muggsy because they both sound exactly the same. (They also sound suspiciously like Turdy and Flaps from the Turdy, Flaps and Mel show just down the dial on a rival station.) But Sue is easy to spot because she's the woman. And even if she had a really deep, mannish voice, you'd still be able to identify her easily because she's always the one saying: 'Oh, Muggseeeee!!' when good ol' Muggsy takes the joke too far.

Sue's only job, her whole raison d'être, is to sit in the studio and rein in those cheeky lads when they get out of control.

Bricko, Muggsy *and* Sue all use 'Don't go there!' and its close relative 'I'm not going there!' with alacrity. It usually starts with one of them, say Muggsy, introducing a topic and setting up a bit of banter.

'Hey Bricko, hey Suze, did you see there's been some research that shows coffee makes you *impotent*!'

This will be followed by a lot of laughter because that's already a pretty funny topic. Limp penises?! Men who can't get hard? What could be funnier at 7.30 a.m.? There must be a hundred jokes you could do about soft cocks. But unfortunately no one has bothered to write any, so instead, once they stop guffawing about how funny this topic *could* be, one of them says, 'I'm not going there, mate!' and then the other one backs him up just in case he was about to change his mind. 'Too right buddy, don't go there! Do *not* go there!'

The implication is that anything they say will be far too edgy so, for the sake of the listeners, they are not going to go there. If they went there, it'd be some seriously dangerous comedy that we, the audience, probably couldn't handle.

I wish they would just go there.

I really want to hear this boundary pushing, witty banter that they so selfishly keep to themselves. I want to live on the edge and see if I can handle it. I bet I can.

I knew I had to break up with Catchphrasey Joe when I started visibly flinching any time someone said, 'How are you?' I'd stand there wincing as I waited for the 'Fine, mild and 27 degrees' bomb to drop.

Unfortunately, at that age, I didn't know how to break up with someone. It's actually a very hard thing to do because you don't want to hurt someone's feelings, even if they do make you want to take a hot glue gun and fill your ears every time they open their mouth. So I'm ashamed to say that I employed the coward's break-up method, which is when you start behaving incredibly poorly and become a really unpleas-ant, unreasonable human being in the hope that the other person will turn around and say, 'Wow, you're awful, I think we should break up.' And then you will get to say, 'Oh no, really? That makes me so sad but if that's what *you* want, then okay, bye!'

The reality is, that rarely happens. Often it backfires completely and the person you're trying to break up with starts being even nicer to you. Like Catchphrasey Joe, who thought he could jolly me out of my foul moods by saying things like, 'Could be worse, we could be dead!'

I kind of wished I was.

Eventually I ended things by announcing that I was moving interstate. He was taken by surprise. As was I. Because I quite literally came up with the idea on the spot, as we were sitting in the pub having a drink. He'd just told the woman behind the bar that he was fine, mild and 27 degrees and I suddenly blurted out that I was moving interstate.

He asked why and I had no answer. I wasn't prepared for a follow-up question. I had nothing, so I improvised, which is not my strong suit. I am a dreadful improviser. Whether I am on stage or in a TV studio, I like to be prepared, I don't like riffing. There is so much pressure on a stand-up comedian to always have a punchline, to always end up somewhere funny, but so often when you're 'just riffing' it goes nowhere. I admire the people that can do it well, it's a rare skill. Many people do it badly, I'm one of those. The worst people, however, are the ones who do it badly but with great confidence, they're the ones who invariably end up saying, 'Ohhhh mate, I'm not going there!'

Sitting in that bar, unaware that I was no good at improvising because I hadn't done any kind of performing yet, I had a go at coming up with a story about why I was moving interstate. Going through my mind was the fact that only a couple of days earlier, Catchphrasey Joe and I had been discussing my career or lack thereof. I had no idea what I wanted to do with my life, write something maybe? Be in advertising maybe? Stay at the Pizza Hut and work my way up to manager? Quite possibly. Frighteningly ambitious I was.

Catchphrasey Joe had been in advertising for over a decade and he really enjoyed playing the wise old owl of the industry. He'd recently told me that one of the best ways to get into the 'ad game' was as a copywriter in a radio station.

It actually wasn't a bad idea and I'd certainly never have thought of it myself. Also, the minute he'd mentioned it, the latent performer in me began to reawaken. I imagined working as a copywriter in a radio station would go something like this:

I'd start out writing the ads but then one day Mel from Turdy, Flaps & Mel would call in sick. The producer would then run into the office in a complete state of panic, yelling, 'We need a woman! We have to keep these guys in line, they're getting out of control! They're all "going there". Someone needs to stop them!'

I'd be in that studio in a jiff, headphones on, being totally awesome and occasionally even 'going there'. Before long it would be Turdy, Flaps and Flanno. That's how I saw it playing out in my mind, not any time soon mind you, just one day, down the track. There was plenty of time, I was young, I'd get onto that radio copywriter thing some day but for the moment, I had a pretty busy shift schedule at the Pizza Hut and those artificial bacon chips at the salad bar weren't going to refill themselves.

So, as I sat in the bar, scratching around for the reason I was moving interstate, the copywriter-in-a-radio-station conversation came back to me, including the bit where he'd said, 'It would be a lot easier to get a start in a regional radio station rather than one of the big city ones.'

So I improvised a story about being inspired by what he'd said a few weeks before and how I'd decided to take his advice and move interstate to get a job in a radio station. It was quite ingenious really, especially considering I came up with it on the fly. I was pretty much making it his fault that we were breaking up, after all it had been his idea for me to move to the regions.

But still his questions kept coming.

Where was I going?

Had I sent off résumés?

Did I need a reference?

Did I have a job already?

Jesus Christ, shutup already, of course I didn't have a job. I hadn't even known I was moving to Western Australia until thirty seconds ago when those words unexpectedly flew out of my mouth. Western Australia? I must have been trying to make sure there was no chance of continuing the relationship long distance.

In hindsight it would have been easier to have just broken down, admitted I was lying and said, 'Sorry Joe, that's all rubbish. I'm not going anywhere, I'm just breaking up with you.' But I didn't want to hurt his feelings and also I've never been one to have my bluff called. I prefer to keep a lie going to the point where it becomes obvious to everyone in the room that I am lying and, not only that, I also know that they know I'm lying, but I still can't stop. Fortunately I never played the game of chicken as a kid, that one where you stand on the road in front of an oncoming car, waiting until the very last moment before you scarper, and the person who holds their nerve and stays out there the longest wins. I'd have been run over for sure, just to prove a point (and win the game).

Determined to see my lie right through to the bitter end, I broke up with Catchphrasey Joe and moved to Western Australia. I'm still not sure why I didn't just break up with him and then 'change my mind' about moving, which would have been a lot easier. But I was only twenty-two and I think my fontanelle was still open.

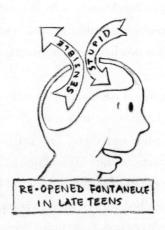

RE·OPENED FONTANELLE
IN LATE TEENS

TWO BIRDS IN A BUNKER

I'd been on the lam in Western Australia, having run away from Catchphrasey Joe several months before, when I finally managed to land a job as a copywriter at an odd little satellite radio station in Bunbury, about two hours' south of Perth. It wasn't a proper radio station in that there was no actual studio and no announcers. No Bricko and Muggsy types, so for the moment my on-air dreams took a backseat.

The station played music, news and ads. And it had a staff of two. Me and another small woman who sat side by side at a single, skinny desk pushed up against the wall in a tiny low-ceilinged, windowless bunker. I think maybe that's why I got the job—because I was small enough to fit in the 'office'.

Our boss sat somewhere else in the large building above us. Somewhere with a window I suspect. We saw him occasionally when he popped his head in to check neither of us had died in the bunker. I think we doubled as the building's canary. Perhaps the whole radio station was a ruse and we were just there to let everyone know when the amount of air in the building dropped to a dangerous level. 'Those two birdlike women in the bunker are having difficulty breathing, everybody out!!'

The whole station was automated, so the most important job was the scheduling, which is what Debbie, the other woman, did. She lined up twenty-four hours of content every day to play in the right order at the right time—the music, the local news, the sheep and wheat reports, and the ads for local businesses. The tricky bit was that the station broadcast all over Western Australia, so Debbie had to schedule different 'newses' and different local business ads to play in each region. No point playing an ad for a butcher up in Kununurra to the people down in the Esperance region. No matter how good the deal was on chump chops, chances were that no one was going to make a 39-hour drive to get them. My job was to write the ads. That was all. Debbie did the hard bit of actually keeping the station running. She was like a human algorithm, she did everything with a pencil and paper working on these giant spreadsheets. Then, once she had it all in order, she'd enter all the data into the computer.

It was a stressful job and Debbie was a stressed-out individual. She always arrived at work in a frenzied state because she'd had to get up at 5 a.m. in order to get her kids off to school, her husband off to work and then clean the whole house from top to bottom. Her morning cleaning regime included vacuuming the house, also from top to bottom. Everything in that house was done from top to bottom. By contrast, the only thing I did every day from top to bottom was put clothes on.

Debbie and I started work the same way every day, with her providing a harried account of how she'd cleaned and vacuumed the whole house from top to bottom before she came to work. It really dominated her life all this top to bottom vacuuming. I didn't even own a vacuum cleaner. Nor did I aspire to own one. It's safe to say that at that age, if you ever actually manage to accumulate enough money to buy a vacuum cleaner, you're not actually going to buy a vacuum cleaner, you're going to do what I did and buy a car instead. Because a car that costs the same as a vacuum cleaner promises to be an incredibly reliable vehicle.

Debbie had so much nervous energy, and she talked about her cleaning schedule with such intensity that I once, jokingly, asked her how often she had to replace her benchtops. She looked at me like I was an idiot. Why would she need to replace her benchtops? They were spotless. I said, 'Yeah, heh heh, but with all that scrubbing you're probably wearing holes in the Laminex!' She didn't laugh. And with good reason. It wasn't particularly funny. In my defence, I wasn't in comedy at that stage.

One morning, in an attempt to make casual chitchat about

her favourite topic—cleaning—I asked her why she didn't get a cleaner. She seemed to spend a lot of her time cleaning, so I figured it might be worth getting a cleaner? Help her get some of her time back? Help her turn up to work not in a foul mood every day.

Debbie's head snapped around and she looked at me like I'd just taken a crap on her spotless Laminex benchtop. She said, 'The day I get a cleaner is the day I give up.' Then she kind of hissed at me. *Ssstt.* So angry. And so weird!

I didn't understand her response at all. Her words made no sense. For me, the day I got a cleaner would be the day I'd made it! And the day I got a driver would be the day I knew I'd died and gone to heaven. That's how you'd get me to be a suicide bomber, tell me there are seventy-two drivers waiting for me in heaven. How I would love to never have to drive anywhere again. To sit in the backseat and be driven around like a non-racist, far more interesting version of that miserable old bat Miss Daisy. Driving Miss Daisy, honestly, if I'd been Morgan Freeman I'd have driven that woman into a lake.

It had been clear from the outset that Debbie and I were from very different backgrounds but this 'cleaner issue' really cemented our non-friendship. From that day on, she took an intense dislike to me. To be fair, I disliked her right back. She was always so tense and stressed. I guess two kids, an unhelpful husband and two full-time jobs would stress anyone out. (I'm counting cleaning as her second full-time job, by the way, in case that wasn't clear.)

I, on the other hand, was having a whale of a time, with the only bad thing about my life being sharing an office with hissy old Debbie. I wrote ads for local businesses in every part of Western Australia, for butchers and stationery shops, hardware stores and pubs including the Roebuck Bay Hotel in Broome, where wet T-shirt competitions were a big drawcard and I didn't have the maturity or good sense to be morally outraged or refuse to include that detail in the ads I was writing.

'Get on down to the Roey, this weekend! Friday it's happy hour from five 'til six and really happy hour from six 'til seven when it's wet T-shirt o'clock! Everybody welcome, and entry is free if you take your top off!! The Roebuck Bay Hotel.'

Hashtag shame on me.

My job was a doddle. The most frustrating part of it was constantly trying (and failing) to convince businesses not to put their phone number at the end of every ad. I was desperately trying to be creative with my work. I saw myself as a serious copywriter and I was convinced I was churning out potentially award-winning ads for local stockfeed sellers. The only thing getting in the way of me and a gold advertising trophy was some pesky business owner insisting I put their phone number at the end of the ad. It still annoys me to this day when I hear an ad on the radio and they give out a phone number. *Nobody* is pulling their car over to write down a phone number. Just say your business name a few times and people will remember that and look it up if they want to find you. Also, is it really necessary to mention that you give friendly advice and offer professional service? Surely those things are standard. It's like when a guy tells me he loves his kids. *Of course* you do, that doesn't make you special, they're *your* kids, you're supposed to love them. My point is that some things are a given and don't need to be mentioned.

I eventually moved back to Sydney after a couple of years in Western Australia, motivated less by the offer of a job in a proper advertising agency and more by the fact that I wanted to break up with someone. I had my tried and tested 'I'm moving away' method by then so I figured it would be a cinch. I sat the man down, put on my saddest face and told him I was really sorry but I was moving back to Sydney. He reached over, took my hands and told me how excited he was because he'd always wanted to move to Sydney. I did not see that one coming. We moved to Sydney together and very quickly I reverted to my back-up break-up method of behaving badly in the hope that he would break up with me. So perverse.

It would be years before I would learn how to break up with someone properly.

DRUG TALK

I have not taken many drugs, so I am not particularly drug literate. I'm not even sure how one refers to drugs. Recently I was leaving a theatre, having just done a show, and one of the other performers was standing outside Stage Door smoking. He offered me a drag (*do you call it a drag?*) on his cigarette which I thought was a bit odd. Who's that desperate they would want a puff (*is it a puff?*) of someone else's germy cigarette? I politely declined, saying, 'No thank you, I don't smoke, never have, so (laugh laugh) I probably won't take it up now!' I'm sure he was grateful for all the extraneous information. Probably thought, *Hey thanks, Mary Whitehouse, self-appointed queen of Wowserville, that's good to know!*

Once we were out of earshot my friend stopped me and said, 'You do realise that was a joint? He wasn't offering you a toke (*dammit, that's the word I should have been using—toke!*) of his cigarette.'

Right. Of course he wasn't. What an idiot. Not that it made that much difference. I'd have said no to a joint as well. I tend not to take drugs because I'm not the sort of person who can just shrug off any annoying drug-related behaviour and say, 'Oh well, who cares? I was wasted, I'm sure people will understand.' Rather, I relive all the annoying things I did over and over to the point where I can't sleep. The next day I almost always feel compelled to do a ring around and apologise to everyone, which is almost as annoying as the annoying drug behaviour.

While most comedians could fill a book with drug stories, I will need just a couple of pages to provide an extensive account of my lame and limited drug-taking history. Let us start with what me and my good friends from Wowserville call the gateway drug.

Marijuana

I am actually fine if I smoke marijuana on my own. I can lie in a dark room and listen to music and have a lovely time. And that is exactly why I choose not to smoke marijuana. I have got shit to do, people. I'm already the world's greatest procrastinator, the last thing I need is a drug that tells me, '*Hey, it's absolutely fine to lie around and do nothing. Relax man, do you know what would solve the world's problems? If everyone just lay back, smoked a joint and listened to music. Because then there'd be no wars. Wow, that's some pretty genius thinking, you should totally get up and write that down and then tomorrow you should send it to the Minister for Fixing the World's Problems.'*

So smoking on my own is a no-go. And smoking with other people is a complete disaster. I never understand the way people just offer you a joint, right off the bat, like that guy did outside the theatre. No pre-joint interview, no responsible service of marijuana. Shouldn't they ask you first what type of stoned person you are? 'Hey before I offer you this, tell me, can you handle weed (*do people call it weed?*) or are you going to freak out and be all paranoid and annoying?'

Because if anyone ever asked me that, I would be obliged to say:

'Put that thing away my friend because if I have any of that pot (*I'm kidding! I know we don't say pot because that's what my mum calls it!*) I am going to be so annoying. I will need all sorts of looking after, my paranoia will go through the roof, and there is every chance I will run off into the bushes believing I am being chased by man-eating porpoises who have legs and can run on land.'

You might well be thinking, hang on, did I miss a bit? Did I turn two pages at once? Is she talking about LSD now? No, I just have a really adverse reaction to marijuana when I am around other people. Once I lost the power of my legs (fortunately it wasn't when those man-eating porpoises were after me).

I was travelling with a super easygoing surfer guy and I wanted to be just like him, I wanted to be super easygoing and a surfer too. So when the bus stopped to let everyone off for a comfort break and he suggested we have a joint, I said, 'Sure! I'm a big ol' joint smoker' and then my legs stopped working. At first it was really funny and he thought I was joking, and admittedly I was laughing pretty hard but in a crazy, panicky way because I genuinely couldn't move my legs. When we saw the driver heading back to the bus, things got a bit more serious, but I still couldn't get up, then we heard the engine start and the 'let's go' horn honk and my easygoing surfer friend got a little less easygoing about my mucking around and a little more urgent about my getting back on the bus. But I couldn't do it. 'Just go,' I said, 'I'll be fine, I'll get the next bus, I'll stay here till my legs start working again. How long does this stuff usually last?' That's when he picked me up, threw me over his shoulder like a sack of potatoes and carried me back to the bus. What a lovely dude! (*Do we say dude?*) Shame I never got his number or I'd have phoned him to apologise for being so annoying.

Speed

I've never taken coke but I have snorted (*is that the word?*) its filthy, made-in-a-biker's-toilet, white-trash cousin called speed. Actually, that's not true, I was too scared to snort it, worrying that the inside divider bit of my nose might fall out. That actually happened to a soap star in England, although to be fair she took coke pretty much all day every day for ten years before she ended up with one single giant nostril. But still, better safe than sorry, so I mixed the dirty putrid powder with some lemonade and drank it. And for the next ten hours I thought I was the most fabulous, gorgeous, fascinating young woman New Year's Eve had ever seen.

The fact is I was none of those things and I am incredibly lucky I didn't get punched in the head or pushed under a train. After ten hours of behaving like a complete cockhead, in public, I lay on the floor at my friend's house for another ten hours and behaved like a cockhead in private, talking *at* her incessantly. I was lucky not to get punched in the head or thrown off a balcony. Never again.

Weird little green pills

To this day, I have no idea what the weird little green pills were. They were given to me at Schiphol Airport in Amsterdam while I was in line waiting to board a plane. As far as I can recall, the person ahead of me in the queue was getting a little antsy, she turned to me and said, 'Oooh gee, not looking forward to this, I'm a really nervous flyer.'

'Yeah, me too,' I replied. This, despite the fact that I am not a nervous flyer. I am, however, a nervous conversationalist and this was my poor attempt at making chitchat—to just agree with her.

The woman, obviously thinking we were now simpatico besties, wanted to do me a favour. 'Here you are, these will help a lot. *Ay-lot!*' she said, tipping four little green pills into my hand.

I cannot tell you how out of character it was for me to accept random pills from a stranger, let alone to go ahead and take them. I didn't pop (*pop? Is that the right word?*) them straight away, I wrapped them in a tissue and put them in my pocket. Then, at some point on the short flight from Amsterdam to Paris, I realised I had weird green pills in my pocket and that I probably didn't want customs asking me what they were. So I took them. It makes no sense. I could have easily thrown them down the toilet and I have no idea why I didn't. Truly, if I saw that scene in a film I'd think, *Well that's just lazy screenwriting, it's not logical, why didn't she just throw them away?*

All I can offer by way of an excuse is that I had been travelling for over thirty-six hours, I'd had little to no sleep and I was slightly delirious. My guess is these pills were some kind of muscle relaxant. Whatever they were, turns out that one would have been ample, and I certainly didn't need four of them. Soon after 'popping' them, I was up at the front of the plane, banging on the cockpit door, telling the pilot to hurry up. Just to clarify, I wasn't telling him to step on it, put his foot down and get us to Paris quick sticks, rather, I thought the cockpit was the bathroom and that I was banging on the door telling whoever was in there to hurry up so I could use the toilet. This, by the way, does not excuse my behaviour, possibly it makes it worse. Who bangs on the dunny door on a plane?

Fortunately for me, this was all pre-9/11 or I'd have been crash-tackled by an air marshal for such behaviour. As it happened, I may as well have been crash-tackled because pretty soon I was lying face down in the aisle. I don't remember exactly how it happened. The flight attendant or 'air waitress lady' as I called her—to her face—patiently led me away from the cockpit door. And I said, 'Thank you, Air Waitress Lady, I think someone might be trapped in there, they've been in there for ages!'

Shortly after that I fell over in the aisle of the plane. (Or maybe I was shoved, which would have been fair enough. Who wants to be referred to as 'Air Waitress Lady'?) There I lay, face down, laughing my head off. I wasn't even in the slightest bit embarrassed, I genuinely thought it was hilarious. And that's when I began to fear the little green pills. Not because I was humiliated by the experience, quite the opposite. It was quite liberating. I was behaving like a total dick but for the first time ever I really didn't care. Fortunately I never found out what those little green pills were, otherwise I might have become addicted to them for life.

Valium

For me, Valium came the closest to replicating the 'I don't-care' factor of the little green pills, in that it stopped me worrying about what everyone was thinking of me. Which was probably nothing. The strange thing about paranoia is that it's almost a form of arrogance because when you're paranoid you're convinced that everyone is thinking about you. Whereas, in reality, people are far too concerned with their own lives to bother wasting time thinking about someone else's boring life that has nothing to do with them.

I used to take Valium on planes—not much, just a bit. I took it because it calmed me down. I'm not afraid of flying but I am afraid of my totally irrational hatred of other passengers and what I might do or say to them. Oddly I am a very calm driver and do not suffer road rage (except when people refuse to give me a courtesy wave for letting them in), however I am obscenely intolerant when travelling on planes. For example, I loathe people who put their seats back on short flights. It's rude and unnecessary and selfish. If you're travelling from Sydney to Melbourne, for an hour and a half, just sit up, don't lie back in my lap. Somewhat surprisingly I don't object to a child kicking the back of my seat. What I vehemently object to, however, is the parent next to the child who does nothing about it.

On long-haul flights I have way too much time to fester about everything everyone is doing wrong. The worst part is that half hour you spend on board before take-off, especially if there is an empty seat next to you. I work myself into an apoplectic state during that thirty minutes trying to will the flight attendant up front to close the door, thinking, oh come on, shut the door while I still have an empty seat next to me, shut it! Shut it! I can't read or concentrate on anything else besides that empty seat and the desperate hope that it might stay empty for the entire flight. Every time a person comes down the aisle I think to myself, *Keep walking, do not sit your fat arse down next to me, just keep walking mister, keep on walking.* And note that when I am in this state 'fat arse' is not a comment on someone's size. You could be a size six but if you look like you're about to take the seat next to me, I want your fat arse to keep on walking.

Taking a few milligrams of Valium before getting on a plane made that pre-take-off half hour so much more peaceful. My psychotic behaviour disappeared, my mind was at rest and I think my face probably relaxed too. Usually it was contorted into a kind of unpleasant gargoyle. I think I was doing it subconsciously to try to repel people. Thanks to Valium, instead of silently seething and working myself into a frenzy over something that might or might not happen, I was now able to look across the aisle with a dazed smile on my face, gazing at the inconsiderate, oblivious parents who were letting their kid play a game on their iPad without headphones. I found the constant diddleedee woodleewoo electronic music and the beebapbow, blip blip, blap blap sound effects as the pig jumped over the sheep and chopped up the farmer with an axe (or whatever the dumb game was) to be quite meditative. In fact, there were times when I'd think, perhaps I should lean over and ask them to turn it up. But in a really warm, fuzzy, genuine way, rather than my typical, angry sarcastic way. 'Yeah, that's not annoying at all, why don't you turn it up? Good parenting, champ, not putting headphones on your kid, don't want to damage its precious ears, don't worry about my ears though, they're already damaged . . . from the noise of your iPad! Then I would laugh without smiling. 'Ha ha ha.' But all that was BV, before Valium.

Valium made me a lovely person to sit next to on a plane. I could really see the appeal of this drug and why women in the fifties and sixties were knocking it back to help them cope with their lives.

And then I ruined it for everyone.

On one particular flight, I had a drink with my Valium to celebrate my new-found status as a delightful, relaxed traveller. Unfortunately, the combination of alcohol and Valium turned me into the most insufferable person on the plane. I was like a grown-up version of that kid who sits behind you repeatedly kicking your seat. Only I doubled down on the bad behaviour by also turning around and peering over the seat at the person behind me like that kid who likes to play peekaboo. But instead of it being a cute two-year-old playing peek-aboo, it was a slurring 35-year-old with a loud nasal voice playing 'chattyfuck'—blathering away at someone who clearly did not want to be talked at.

The friend I was travelling with kept tapping me, quite hard, and saying, 'Mate! Stop it. Turn around, they're not interested, you're being annoying.'

Wow. What a buzzkill she was. And she had no idea what she was talking about. I was pretty sure everyone on the plane was *loving* me! Especially the 'Air Waitress Man', who had a villa in Spain and didn't even object to the fact that I called him 'Air Waitress Man' to his face. Maybe he'd had some Valium too. He gave me his number and told me to call him and we made grand plans to meet up somewhere in Spain. (You may have noticed by now that I make a lot of grand plans.) I told my friend, and most of the plane, about my new-found friend and how we were going to get together in some Spanish back-water no one had ever heard of. My friend took the piece of paper with his number on it and offered to hold on to it for safekeeping. Later on, she ripped it up in front of me, which was a real shame. I always think about what could have been if I'd kept his number and managed to meet up with Air Waitress Man at his villa/rape dungeon. I could be dead right now or at the very least I could have given him a ring and apologised for calling him Air Waitress Man.

BRIDGE BURNING IN SINGAPORE

I'd only been doing stand-up comedy for about six months when I was offered a four-week residency at a comedy club in Singapore.

It was an unbelievable offer. At that stage of my non-existent career I was doing open-mic nights and occasional, paid fifteen-minute spots. I could hardly call myself a comedian. I was still more of a copywriter, sort of. About a year before, I'd been made redundant from my advertising agency job due to a merger. They said they had to 'let me go' because I was the most recent hire, the old 'last in, first out' argument. Maybe it was true. Personally I think it was more likely that I was 'let go' because I wasn't very good and worse than that, I had no idea I wasn't very good. In fact, I thought I was pretty great.

I'm actually surprised I lasted as long as I did considering the rubbish I was churning out. I remember one particular ad for Nestle Quik, some half-baked idea about a planet made of chocolate powder featuring giant 'spoon' buggies and a jingle about the 'mothership' bringing the milk. Good god, I didn't even have the excuse that I was on drugs. Maybe the client was, I can't think of any other reason he would have approved such garbage. I'll guarantee Quik sales didn't go through the roof that year.

Since my 'letting go', I'd been earning a living as a freelancer writing advertorials for magazines. Those are the ads that are made to look like editorial content in order to trick people into reading them. The idea is you'll be halfway through the 'article', having suffered seventeen casual mentions of Glad Wrap, before you think, *Hang on a minute, this isn't a story about picnics at all! It's about Glad Wrap! Man, they tricked me! But you know what, this Glad Wrap stuff sounds terrific, I'm going to buy some, perhaps in the new sixty-metre catering pack with a never-fail, extra-sharp cutting bar!*

Whether at a radio station, a multinational agency, or working for magazines, my entire time in advertising was wholly unremarkable; not surprisingly, I never did win any of those gold trophies. The upside, at least, was that writing advertorials paid a lot better than stand-up did, certainly at my level.

There were only two proper comedy clubs in Sydney so it was hard to get much stage time and despite what people who run 'comedy courses' will try to tell you, the only way to learn how to do stand-up comedy is by doing it. Lots of it. You don't need a course, you just need stage time, you need to gig as often as possible. So the idea that I would be in Singapore working every night of the week, sometimes doing two shows a night, for four weeks in a row *and* getting paid was unbelievable. I was pretty sure I'd made it, so I called the woman I wrote advertorials for and told her to shove her Mudd Masks and Glad Wrap up her arse. Not really. Thank god I wasn't that stupid. Cos I'd be back in four weeks and once again advertorials would be my main source of income. Singapore didn't quite launch me on to the world comedy stage the way I thought it would.

The comedy club in Singapore was part of a brand new three-storey complex in the tidy (most of Singapore is tidy) touristy area of Boat Quay. On the ground floor there was an English-style pub, the top floor was a karaoke bar and on the middle floor was the comedy club. That's what the sign outside said anyway. In reality you had an English-style pub on the ground floor, a karaoke bar on the top floor and in the middle, where the comedy club was supposed to be, there was a holding pen for all the people who wanted to do karaoke upstairs but couldn't get in because it was so popular.

Karaoke was, by far, the entertainment of choice. Everyone wanted to sing along to that distinctive, high-pitched, twangy wailing that is Mandarin Pop. Couples especially loved it. And for a culture obsessed with dignity and not losing face, there seemed to be an awful lot of lost face happening as couples caterwauled and keened across at least three octaves as they covered a bit of Wanfang or A-mei (by all accounts these two Taiwanese singers are still top of the pops when it comes to Singaporean karaoke). Where Australians like to do a bit of 'Khe Sanh', Singaporeans prefer Wanfang, a power-bal-lad-type singer in the style of Celine Dion, if you can imagine Celine belting in Chinese instead of Canadian.

So popular was the karaoke bar that it couldn't hold everyone, so instead couples would go in, choose their song, take a number and then come downstairs to wait in the comedy club where there were plenty of empty seats. Plenty. Con-veniently, they installed an intercom–speaker system in the comedy club so that the karaoke hostess upstairs could call people's numbers to let them know when it was time to come on up, grab the mic and start ripping out their best Wanfang. In that way it was not unlike being in an Australian RSL club, only instead of constant announcements about schnitzels being ready it was abrupt Mandarin being barked through a crackling PA system ordering people up to the karaoke bar. Obviously I don't speak Mandarin but I always imagined they were saying, 'Hey! Hey! Couple 42. Get upstairs. Quick! Get out of that stupid comedy club right now. Save yourselves. Couple 42. Couple 42. You have ten seconds. If you have a drink, please throw it at the unfunny foreigner on stage before you leave. Couple 42. Time to sing. Time to shine. Let's go, let's go!'

There were three of us on the comedy club bill. I was the least experienced, and far more 'comedian in training' than proficient stand-up. I was lucky to be there. My act—if you could call it that—was decent by beginner comedian standards, but woeful by professional comedian standards. The other two were proper full-time comics. The three of us worked six nights a week, two shows a night on the weekends, usually to about half a dozen unsuspecting tourists who'd wandered in off the street and foolishly sat down at a table before they realised it wasn't necessarily 'comedy' as they knew it. By the time they worked it out they often didn't have the heart to leave.

Any time I ever find myself watching some tedious theatre production and wishing I could walk out, I think back to my time in Singapore and the generosity those audience members showed by not leaving. They were just decent people, on holiday, out to have a good time, and then they made the simple mistake of walking into a comedy club expecting to see some comedy. Instead what they got was a bizarre piece of performance art. One corner of the room tightly packed with dozens of silent Singaporean couples, all of them staring at the speaker on the wall willing it to squawk their number. And in the other corner, on a slightly raised dais, a panicky, sweaty, frizzy-haired Australian woman spewing out 'jokes' so fast you could barely understand them. Bless those holiday-makers for not walking out and adding to my humiliation. It was very kind of them to stay and suffer along

123

with me. Some would say that sort of experience is character building and I'm sure it is, but it's also soul destroying.

When I wasn't busy punishing half a dozen unfortunate punters with my comedy or visiting Singapore's tourist attraction (not a typo, there was only one) I was back at the accommodation. The arrangement was that the three comics all shared a three-bedroom apartment in a tower block about twenty minutes' drive out of town. My comedian flatmates for the month were two guys. One was so pale-skinned he had no business going out during daylight hours. He was white to the point of translucence and the sun was his sworn enemy. Honestly, a twenty-watt globe would have burned his skin. I think he went out on his first day in Singapore, blistered himself stupid, and then stayed indoors for the rest of the time. On the rare occasions he had to leave the building, he would slather himself in an unholy amount of sunscreen that was so thick it looked like he was covered in goose fat and preparing to swim the English Channel.

The other comedian staying in the apartment was a real bon vivant, or maybe he was a sociopath, I'm still not sure. He told stories of living in Rwanda and having oral sex with a pygmy lady. He even got tears in his eyes as he remembered the utter joy he'd brought to this simple tribeswoman as he 'pleasured her with his tongue'—his words, not mine. He'd also spent a bit of time running opium for Thai drug lords. Apparently.

At the end of my four weeks of purgatory, I sat in a restaurant having lunch with the two Singaporean men who owned the club. They said they were keen to hear my thoughts and get some feedback. What they didn't say was that they were only keen to hear those thoughts if they went something like this: 'Wow. Best comedy club ever. Two thumbs up. Thanks guys, you really know how to do comedy in Singapore. I hope you'll invite me back, I've really loved my time here!'

Fortunately, I'd been warned by the Australian booker of the club not to be sucked in by their 'we would love to hear your honest feedback' act. *Do not*, under any circumstances, she'd said, give them constructive criticism. It would not be well received. To be criticised by a Western woman would amount to a severe loss of face, and losing face is a big thing in Singapore. No one wants to lose their face.

So instead I put on my best fake smile and, as instructed, kept my feedback light and positive, not saying anything negative, which was a bit of a strain considering the difficult four weeks I'd just had. I said how much I'd loved the experience and made general chitchat about how great Singapore was. I conveniently forgot to congratulate them on how successful their government had been in repressing homosexuality. The Singaporean government takes a very simple approach to homosexuality and just refuses to admit it exists. That's why there's no gays there. None at all.

The lunch was going pretty well until one of the club owners leant over, stroked my face and said, 'Kitty, why do you have a moustache?'

Now, if he'd said that to me on the first day, I probably would have laughed it off and said something like, 'Oh come on, get out of here, you big silly!'

But I had been on my absolute best behaviour for twenty-nine days, I had held it together and hadn't snapped at anyone the whole time, even on day six when I sat down next to a Singaporean woman on the bus and she looked at me then screwed her nose up and sniffed in my general direction several times, all the while rapidly wafting her hand back and forth in front of her face. Pretty much the only thing she didn't do was shout, 'Pyew, you stink!' But then again, she didn't need to, the gesture was fairly unambiguous. When I recounted what had happened to the locals who worked behind the bar at the comedy club I was reliably informed that most Westerners smell funny to Singaporeans, largely due to the amount of dairy in our diet. And I eat more dairy than most. Cheese and yoghurt are my main vices along with flavoured milk. So it's reasonable to assume I really did stink like old blue cheese. I chose to view the bus incident as a cultural learning moment rather than something to be offended by.

On day eleven, I'd again demonstrated remarkable restraint when I went into a pharmacy and was offered a product that would help shrink my massive vagina. To be clear, I had not asked for this product nor had I declared that I was suffering from MVS (Massive Vagina Syndrome), I simply wanted something to manage my acne and I'd heard about this supposed herbal remedy you could get in Singapore. However, the pharmacist wisely saw beyond my skin condition to a much bigger issue. Literally. He waved away my request for a herbal acne treatment and told me, not quietly, what my real problem was.

'Western women have very big vaginas,' he said. Then he produced a jar of magic vagina-shrinking powder and held it out to me, 'Use this to make small, make husband happy.' Those were his very words. And he was obviously concerned that I might not understand what he was saying (possibly due to the echo being created by the enormous cave I had between my legs) so he added some none-too-subtle mime work, making a large circle with his two hands, about ten centimetres in diameter, which I recognised immediately as my offensively over-sized female 'area'. He told me to apply the powder to the offending area, miming dab dab dab (I only hoped he had enough in stock, I mean a fanny like mine was going to absorb a lot of that magic minge dust) and then voila! He closed his hand circle down to a far more desirable teeny-tainy size. Again, I took neither offence nor umbrage. I just nodded and ruefully told him that I didn't have a husband (no doubt because of my cavernous lady hole!) so I was not in the market for his special shmoo-shrinking powder. He eventually sold me some pills for my acne. Later on, while reading the information leaflet, I discovered those pills contained armadillo testicles. And for anyone thinking of eating armadillo testicles to get rid of acne, don't bother, they don't work, let the poor armadillo keep his nuts.

So to recap, during my stay in Singapore, I'd been told I was stinky and that I had a fanny you could drive a truck through. I'd accidentally eaten god knows how many armadillo testicles and couldn't find a relevant charity for armadillo eunuchs anywhere, which meant I had no way to assuage my guilt. On top of that, the 90 per cent Singaporean humidity had turned me into a sweaty, human tumbleweed and all the while I was sharing a flat with a goose-grease-covered ghost and a pygmy-licking something-o-path. Is it any wonder that by lunchtime on my last day I'd finally hit breaking point? That's why, when the owner touched my face and asked, 'Why do you have a moustache?' I slapped at his hand and said, 'Why are you such a cunt?'

Reflecting on this now, I see that not only did I overreact, it's also a very poor comeback, there's nothing clever about it at all. Worse than that, it's totally reliant on shock value, which is my least favourite type of comedy.

Curiously, it sparked no reaction whatsoever from either owner. Neither of them reared back and said, 'How dare you?!' or 'Madam! Language!' or 'That's some pretty rude talk for a smelly lady with a big box.' They just smiled (a little tightly) and I assumed my comment had been taken as a bit of light-hearted joshing around. I was a comedian after all. (I wasn't, I was still very much a copywriter.) Point is, everything seemed fine, lunch was over, we all shook hands and said goodbye. As we were saying our farewells, I remembered to ask whether someone would be coming to pick me up the next day to take me to the airport. Of course, they said. That was part of the deal.

No one came. I rang the office to find out what was happening. 'Oh yes,' I was told, 'they're on their way.' They weren't. And I almost missed my flight, which would have been a disaster. I couldn't afford to buy a new plane ticket and the club certainly wouldn't have paid for another one. More to the point, I couldn't afford to spend one more day in Singapore in the state I was in. I was clearly losing my mind and I had to get out.

I learned later, not that I hadn't already guessed, that I had been 'deleted'. Because of my hugely insulting behaviour, I no longer existed. It was all about losing face. The thing is, I'm not sure if I'd lost face because I'd behaved so poorly or if the club owner had lost face because I'd insulted him in front of a colleague. All I know is that one of us doesn't have a face anymore. Both of us, however, still have a moustache.

PART THREE

THE GRAVEDIGGER'S WIFE, THE STONER'S PROSTITUTE AND OTHER FAILED ROMANCES

A BIT OF A DICK

Six weeks in South America is an ambitious first trip for anyone, let alone a couple who have only been together for a few months. But that's where my new boyfriend wanted to go and I was a joiner, and an incredible optimist it seems. This was pre-internet, pre-smartphone and pre-South America being a relatively easy and popular tourist destination for English speakers with zero Spanish language skills.

Ever the conscientious swot, I attempted to learn some Spanish before we left. This meant going to visit a random, middle-aged, Chilean woman whose number I had torn off a noticeboard in a cafe. 'Learn espanish in my home from a true-life native espeaker!' This woman, Nalia, wasn't a teacher but she sure was a true-life native speaker and so that was the teaching method she employed. She native-spoke at me. That was it. Once a week I would sit in her kitchen listening to her prattle away in espanish for an hour. Occasionally she would pause mid-jabber and say, 'Entiende?' while raising her eyebrows and nodding encouragingly at me. Apparently 'Entiende?' meant 'Do you understand?' I didn't, but she was nodding so I thought it was only polite to nod back. Her idea, I think, was that I would somehow learn espanish by osmosis. I didn't. Although she did once send me home with a little picture book that looked like something one of her kids might have borrowed from the library back in Chile (and forgotten to return) and I definitely absorbed all of that. It was an odd story about a dog that jumped up on a table. I don't want to spoil the ending for you but to this day I still know the Spanish for: 'Hey! The dog is on the table! Hand me my gun.' It's not a sentence I've used often, either in Spanish or English. And when I say often, I mean ever.

Because it was the nineties, all my pre-trip research had to be done using Lonely Planet guidebooks. I had one for every country we planned to visit and I pored over them, making notes and highlighting important information about where to stay, what to do and how to say, 'May I please have my guinea-pig kabob without the head?'

As neither I nor my boyfriend had ever travelled overseas before, I thought we should probably pre-book a hotel for our first night so we had somewhere to go when we arrived in Chile. Booking accommodation was actually a fairly monumental task without the internet. I had to make an international call from Australia to some cheap hotel in Santiago and conduct a conversation in my non-existent espanish but I thought it was a worthwhile and sensible idea, so I did it.

My boyfriend, however, thought it was unnecessary and a great way to ruin our upcoming adventure. I should have seen the red flag in front of my face right then, it was obvious we were not going to travel well together. I am a planner and he was one of those (reeeeeeally annoying) types who like to 'wing it'. In his mind, I was a tourist and he was a traveller. Booking hotels and making plans was something a lame tourist, like me, would do, whereas a traveller, like him, just went with the flow. 'Whatever happens, happens, man.' A traveller doesn't take guidebooks in his 'backpack', a traveller carries a copy of Kerouac's *On the Road* in his 'knapsack'. You dig? Now I'm all for being a spontaneous man of the world and going with the flow but it works a lot better if you are well travelled, worldly wise and, most importantly, fluent in espanish. He was none of those things.

No surprise then that the trip was a complete disaster from start to finish, not only because of the differences in our approach to travel but also because he was a bit of a dick.

One of his constant refrains throughout the trip was, 'Can you please stop trying to speak Spanish because I'm sure their English is better than your Spanish.'

He had a point, my Spanish was woeful, but really, it's a bit of a dick thing to say. Also, I'd read my multitude of guidebooks from cover to cover and I don't remember any of them saying, 'When travelling in a foreign country, it is always better not to attempt the local language. Rather, you should arrogantly swan around like some kind of colonial invader shouting at people in English.'

There was also the time we arrived at a refugio (which is the Spanish word for hostel-in-the-middle-of-freakin'-nowhere) and discovered there were no blankets on the beds—you either brought your own sleeping bag or you could hire one from the refugio office. However, we'd arrived fairly late in the day, by which stage there was only one sleeping bag left for hire.

Ever the gentleman, my boyfriend said, 'Do you mind if I have the sleeping bag? You're small, you can sleep under our coats.'

Technically he was correct, I am small and I can (and did) sleep under our coats. But still, it was a bit of a dick thing to suggest.

It really is my own fault though, I should have seen the writing on the wall before we even left Australia. All the signs were there that this was not going to work out.

The first issue was money. We only took traveller's cheques (I know! How quaint! Remember those?). I'd been worried about not having any local currency on arrival so I suggested we go to the bank and order a small amount of Chilean pesos. He rolled his eyes at such a touristy thought. 'Relax,' he said, 'we can sort the money thing out when we get there.'

Turned out we couldn't 'sort the money thing out' when we got there because we arrived on a bank holiday, ATMs didn't exist yet and everything was closed, including the currency exchange place at the airport. We needed to get from the airport to the city somehow, but as we soon discovered, local buses in Chile don't take traveller's cheques. Luckily there was a little old lady on the bus who saw me ready to burst into tears (good god, again with the crying?!) and must have understood the situation. Maybe she too went out with a bit of a dick in her youth? She took some coins from her little-old-lady purse and pressed them in to my hand, effectively covering our fares to the city. My boyfriend looked at me and said, 'See, I told you it'd be fine. Just relax.' I wasn't sure if I was more annoyed by being told to relax (again) or because he'd been right.

It was late afternoon by the time we finally made it to our hotel after a long circuitous bus ride followed by an even longer walk.

This was the hotel I had painstakingly booked by calling ahead from Australia and pretty much shouting the date and 'Bed! Bed please! Two persons!' in Spanish down the phone. The fact that the hotel owner actually had my name (well, I assume I was Mrs Flamgam, and apologies to the actual Mrs Flamgam if I stole your reservation) and arrival date written down was some kind of miracle. I was high on my own travel awesomeness and feeling very much like a true-life native espeaker, having managed to pull off such a coup. But then my boyfriend's inner dick kicked in and he said, 'Let's go somewhere else.' He didn't like our hotel room, something about the bedspread and the overall vibe 'wasn't great'.

A brief note about our budget at the time. Nowhere we could afford was going to be 'great'. The best we could hope for was 'clean and available' and this place was both. It didn't have bedbugs—something we'd get to enjoy later on in the trip. It didn't have an entire set of toenails littered throughout the bed—another treat we still had to look forward to. Nor did it have an old man hiding in a cupboard in the hallway guarding the bathroom. That came much later on when we stayed at a place where showers cost extra. Apparently some wily, budget-conscious travellers used to pay for a room only, then get up in the middle of the night and try to sneak a free shower but not on his watch! He'd spring out of that cupboard shouting, 'No ducha! No ducha!' and throw himself in front of the doorway, physically barring entry to the bathroom. What a full and satisfying life he led.

My boyfriend suggested we 'go for a bit of a wander' to see if we could find something better. 'Go for a bit of a wander' is a phrase that still makes my stomach spontaneously produce acid.

The hotel owner was on my side. She said, 'There isn't much around here, and if you leave now your room will go. I cannot hold it for you.'

(She said all that in Spanish, so it took about fifteen minutes to get the gist of it, but, no question, the gist was

'There is nothing else out there, this is as good as it gets', a bird in 'la mano' and all that jazz.)

My boyfriend didn't believe her. He thought she was playing us because we were a pair of stupid tourists who didn't know any better. She didn't realise he was a cool, spontaneous traveller who liked to wing it.

'Let's go,' he said.

Several hours and much wandering around later, we ended up back at that hotel asking if our room was still available. What a surprise when the owner said, 'No. Lo siento.'

I translated for my boyfriend. 'She says, no, sorry.'

Annoyed, he said, 'Yes, I got that. Ask her if she knows if there's anywhere else around here that might have a room available, somewhere not too expensive but not, you know, crappy.'

I stared at him incredulous. That was a pretty complex sentence he wanted translated. Clearly at this early stage of the trip he was still vastly overestimating my ability to speak Spanish. I wanted to say, 'Oh come on, seriously? I took one class a week for six weeks so unless you just need a few basic words or there happens to be a dog on the table that needs shooting, I can't help you.'

Instead, I turned to the woman and, in my toddler-like Spanish, said, 'Um . . . hotel another . . . room is there . . . small walking . . . more hotel with room . . . maybe but small walking not big walking?' (Small walking was the best I could do for 'nearby'.)

'What did you ask her?'

'I'm not sure.'

'I thought you could speak Spanish.'

I thought, *I can speak it more than you can, dickhead.*

The hotel owner was surprisingly sympathetic to our dilemma and mimed that she would make a telephone call for us. What a nice lady. If I'd been her, I would have told us to take our arrogant attitude to her bedspreads and 'overall vibe' and get out.

After a few minutes, she was back with what seemed to be good news. She drew a map and gave us directions. After some 'small walking', we arrived at the creepiest looking place I'd ever seen. It was *The Addams Family* house if the Addams Family had been mass murderers rather than a kooky bunch of non-murdering misfits. This 'hotel' clearly rented out rooms, by the hour, to prostitutes and/or serial killers. I wondered which of those we looked like (maybe one of each) as we knocked on a giant set of double wooden doors, the likes of which you would only ever see on a castle. A castle where you might go to die.

A little hatch in one of the doors popped open, a woman's face appeared and hissed at us, 'Passaporte.'

By now I'd been on a plane, a bus, I'd taken charity from an old lady, walked for miles, had lengthy discussions in Spanglish and then 'gone for a bit of a wander'. I'd also barely eaten all day and I was standing outside the *Amityville Horror* house expecting to die soon. So it's hardly surprising that

I panicked when I heard the word 'Passaporte!' I was delirious and I thought she was asking us for a password. I clutched at my boyfriend's arm and said, 'Shit, we didn't get the password. Did you get the password? I don't remember the password!'

I was so tired I couldn't even see how stupid it was to think we would need a password to enter a hotel. She hissed it again, louder this time, 'Passaporte', and I finally realised she wanted our passports. And like idiots who'd never been in a foreign country before, we passed our most valuable documents, along with a traveller's cheque for way too much money, through the hatch. After waiting for what seemed like an age, eventually one of the big castle doors swung open revealing a small woman with very yellow hair who gestured for us to follow her.

The woman said nothing as she led us up a clanging metal staircase. The walls were painted gloss black—I assumed to hide any blood that might have been dripping down them. There were signs up everywhere indicating that electrocution was imminent. That's what I took them to mean, anyway. I'm not sure how else you translate a sign showing lots of lightning bolts radiating from an electricity tower alongside a stick figure spasming with electric shock. It wasn't clear exactly what caused the electrocution but we decided not to touch anything. At all.

We walked into 'our room', and it was only because I was now frightened beyond speech that I couldn't summon up a sarcastic, 'Oh, well this is *so* much better than the place I organised with the daggy bedspreads and the lame vibe!'

The room also had gloss black walls, they seemed to be a hotel standard, maybe gloss black paint had been on special. There was a round bed made up with black sheets and a green chenille coverlet, it was rumpled and looked vaguely slept in. There was also a mirror on the black ceiling and a hot pink, faux-fur rug on the floor, much of it matted and stuck together, maybe with blood, maybe with jizz. It was hard to tell in the ten-watt lighting.

We were busy taking it all in, enjoying the all-important fkn vibe, when there was a knock at the door. I nearly crapped my pants. But it was only Ol' Yella Hair come to return our passports. She'd clearly photocopied them and now had everything she needed to create fake IDs for her serial killer pals who were tired of all the killing and wanted to make a fresh start.

It was impossible to sleep. For a start we couldn't possibly lie down on that Petri dish of a bed. Who knew what was crawling around in there? Plus, we'd decided it was important to be alert and ready to run, lest someone kick the door in, stab us to death, wrap us in the jizz-covered rug and throw us down the electrified stairs.

At dawn, still wide awake having not slept at all, we crept out of our room and tiptoed down the stairs, careful not to touch anything. The signs weren't the only constant reminder of the risk of electrocution, there was also a constant, very loud buzzing noise that made me wonder whether the hotel wasn't built on top of a substation.

The big castle doors at the entrance presented a problem because one of us had to throw open the metal bolt—which we were pretty sure, given the circumstances, was going to be electrified. We had an urgent, whispery fight about who would do it and, if memory serves, it was one of my small victories of the trip. My boyfriend opened the door and we sprinted out into the early morning. We slowed down only once the hotel was out of sight and we were sure Señora Yellow Hair wasn't coming after us with an axe. I'm not entirely sure why we thought she'd come after us, or why we thought she'd have an axe—we were beyond rational thought by that stage.

We then went for 'a bit of a wander' around the empty streets of Santiago while we waited for somewhere to open so we could have some breakfast and commence the exhausting task of looking for another hotel, preferably one that wasn't mentioned in my guidebook. After all, we didn't want to be touristy hacks and stay in the same places everyone else stayed in. We wanted to find somewhere unique and authentic, somewhere with the right bedspread and the right vibe.

In case you're wondering why on earth I stuck it out for the whole six weeks and didn't just up and leave and carry on alone, there were actually two reasons. Number one: this was my first ever overseas trip and I simply didn't have the self-confidence, the experience or, indeed, the bravado to travel by myself. At some point in my twenties, I'd lost my nerve and, with it, my ability to do stupid but adventurous things. That free-wheeling spirit had been replaced by an irrational fear of being raped and murdered, so there was no way I could travel around South America on my own. In my mind that seemed tantamount to putting a sign on my back that said, 'rape and murder me now, ask me how'. The second reason I stayed is far more tragic and says volumes about me and the bad choices I've made over the years. This man was funny. Proper, proper funny. He could make me laugh hard. And that has always been a real problem for me. I'm such a sucker for funny. I absolutely love being around funny people. Even when that funny person is a bit of a dick. So maybe it's actually me who's a bit of a dick.

LIST MAN

I admire people who can just end a relationship. Cut it off clean. No backsliding, no letting themselves be convinced to give things another go, no getting a bit lonely a few days later and calling 'to check in'. They just end it. That's what List Man did.

List Man was super organised about breaking up, compiling a list of all my defects and shortcomings and then reading them out to me. That was his method. At the time it seemed a little harsh, but in retrospect I can see that he was just being efficient. None of that on-again, off-again rubbish for List Man, he knew what he wanted and he wanted out. So one night, after dinner (credit to him, he did the washing-up first) he informed me that we were breaking up. Straight out like that—'We have to break up.' He didn't even warm up to it with the standard break-up warning phrase: 'We need to talk.'

I was shocked. I don't know why. We weren't very well suited, we didn't have much in common, and to be honest I'd been wondering myself exactly how much longer we could continue pretending. It was actually very good of him to call an end to things, otherwise we might have trundled along making each other miserable for another couple of years. The right thing for me to do would have been to behave like a grown-up and say, 'Oh, good on you. Well done, thanks for making it happen. Okay, now let's divide up our things and never see each other again!'

Instead I let my ego get in the way and, somewhat irrationally, found myself being hurt and offended that this person (whom I didn't want to be with anymore) got in first and said he didn't want to be with *me* anymore. Yet another example of the stupidity of humans. I'd been unhappy for a long time and now he was handing me a get-out-of-jail-free card, so it made total sense to throw that card back in his face, burst into tears and wail, 'What? No! I don't understand? What do you mean? Can't we fix things?' and then the dumbest question of all—'Why?'

And that was the question he'd been waiting for because that's when the list came out. He'd clearly been involved in messy break-ups before and this time he was taking no chances. This was going to be a clean, fact-based break-up.

The list included everything from your stock standard relationship complaint of there not being enough sex—just once I'd like to hear of a couple who broke up because they had too much sex—to far more obscure things such as my insane ranting about him coming home one day with a packet of square ham.

My issue was twofold. Firstly, ham shouldn't come in a 'packet', it should be wrapped in deli paper, the stuff they use *at the deli* where one should be buying one's ham. Secondly, ham comes from the hindquarters of a pig and therefore it should be hindquarter shaped. When I see a pig walking around on four solid, square stumps I will happily eat square ham. Until then I believe ham should be a roundish but irregular shape, much like a pig's arse.

Most of his break-up list, including the square ham issue, I couldn't really contest. So what if he liked his ham to fit right to the edges of his square Tip Top bread? It actually makes good sense to combine square bread, square ham and a slice of square cheese. It makes the perfect sandwich with no filling void anywhere. The ham and the cheese go right to the edges all the way around so that every single mouthful delivers an even amount of bread, ham and cheese. More importantly, why did I even care? I didn't have to eat the square ham sandwiches, it's not like he was making them for my lunch every day.

If I had to find fault with his list, I'd say he needed to throw in a couple of mea culpas just to give the illusion of balance. As it was, it was pretty one sided—he clearly believed this break-up was all my fault. I thought it would have been a nice gesture to add one or two 'And I guess I haven't been easy to live with either, what with my insisting on buying square ham all the time' type statements. Just a couple of things to even the score. Although that might have been hard because his own behaviour was fairly exemplary. He didn't really do much wrong except not laugh at anything I said. Ever. And no doubt he saw that as my failing not his. The reason he didn't laugh was because I wasn't funny.

And that would've been fine under normal circumstances. I understand that humour is subjective and not everyone finds the same things funny. However, as a professional comedian, who gets paid cash money to be funny, I found his layperson's opinion rather galling. He concurred that other people might find me funny ('might') but his problem, he said, was that he had a very unique sense of humour. I guess that could be true, in a world where unique means non-existent. Imagine if he'd been dating a chef and said, 'I'm not really enjoying this de-licious, expertly prepared meal you've made. I might whip up a square ham and cheese sandwich with filling that goes right to the edges instead. No offence, I'm sure other people like your cooking but I just have a very unique palate.'

Other transgressions on the list included my not attending his work functions. I felt bad when he mentioned this because I hadn't realised it was a big deal. He would ask me to come along and I would say, 'No thanks' and he would say, 'Okay'. So I assumed he didn't care and that he probably secretly wished he was me so that he didn't have to go either. Who likes work functions? Gatherings where people say things like 'happy wife, happy life' and refer to their respective partners as 'hubby' or 'my old lady' or, god forbid, 'the old ball and chain'. Oh please. I hope they're serving mini kebabs at this 'do' because I might need to puncture my own eardrums with a skewer.

The only item on the list that stuck out as unfathomable was Number 22: 'You spend too much time with your sister.' And that might have been a problem were it not for the fact that my sister is totally awesome.

Overall (with the exception of Number 22) I think it was a fairly well-deserved pasting and once he'd finished his oration he handed me the list for review. That's when I realised I had successfully (but totally unwittingly) employed the coward's break-up method. My behaving badly had driven him to end the relationship. I admit there was a slight thrill at first as I realised that I wasn't being dumped here, I was actually the one doing the dumping, albeit in a perverse roundabout kind of a way. But then as I looked down the list and reviewed what a dreadful person I'd been for the last twelve months, I vowed to avoid that method in future.

THE NOBLE ARSEHOLE

The right way to end a relationship is also the most difficult way. I have managed it only once in my lifetime. I was dating a man who was very funny and kind, but he was also a stoner who didn't get up until about one in the afternoon and that didn't exactly fit in with my lifestyle which, while not exactly a frenzy of activity, has always involved being up to enjoy at least some part of the first half of the day.

Eventually I realised there was no real future in this relationship. I go away a lot for work and I imagined 'our family' at home, all lying in till 1 p.m. when Mr Mom would finally crawl out of bed and take the kids to school just in time for them to catch the bus home.

The real problem for us, however, was that we couldn't

discuss things properly due to his use of 'stoner logic'. Stoner logic is very hard to argue with because it makes no sense. Here is a classic example:

ME: I wish you wouldn't light a joint every 'morning' (*at 1 p.m.*) as soon as you get up.

HIM: But you eat muesli every morning when you get up. It's the same thing.

ME: What? No it isn't. How is it the same? Muesli is food. And it's good for you. A joint is not good for you. Especially not every morning!

HIM: Okay, but how would you feel if I said, 'Hey I've decided you can't eat muesli when you get up tomorrow morning.' Is that fair?

ME: But . . . it's not the same . . . How can you not see that muesli and a joint are two very different things?

HIM: But is it fair to say you can't eat muesli?

ME: No. It's not fair.

HIM: You see? Same thing.

It was like being on the witness stand and being cross-examined by the Caterpillar from *Alice in Wonderland*. Only I think the Caterpillar made more sense and probably wasn't as stoned.

The other very memorable example of stoner logic happened during our break-up, which went like this:

ME: I'm really sorry but this isn't working, I don't want to
go out with you anymore.

I was very direct because I'd learned that you mustn't be
cryptic or leave things open to interpretation when talking to
a stoner.

His eyes immediately grew red and he got very emotional.
Like I said, he was a lovely man, very in touch with his feelings.
Or maybe he was just stoned.

HIM: Are you serious?

ME: Yes. I just don't think we're a good match.

HIM: Oh my god, you need to get over the dope smoking
thing. Everybody smokes. You're the weird one.

ME: Okay, yes, I'm the weird one. I agree.

At this point, I'm going to edit a lot of the conversation out
because it got a little hysterical for about twenty minutes, with
tears on both sides, and eventually when he realised I was
not going to change my mind his patent-pending Stoner Logic
went into overdrive.

HIM: I cannot believe you are doing this now.

ME: What do you mean, now?

HIM: Why couldn't you break up with me a month ago.

ME: I don't know.

HIM: You let me go to Thailand for ten days. You should
have told me you were planning to break up with me.

ME: Well firstly, I haven't exactly been planning it. I've been thinking about it, I guess, but not 'planning' it. Secondly, what's Thailand got to do with it?

HIM: I could have slept with someone in Thailand but I didn't because I was being faithful to you. Now I think what was the point?

ME: Sorry, I'm confused, are you angry with me because we're breaking up or because I robbed you of the chance to sleep with a prostitute?

HIM: She was not a prostitute!!

ME: Really? And this was in Thailand? And she was Thai?

HIM: Yes but not every woman in Thailand is a prostitute.

ME: I couldn't agree with you more, what I'm saying is every woman in Thailand *who wants to sleep with a white man* is a prostitute. Anyway, who cares? I'm still confused. What are you annoyed about?

HIM: I was faithful to you.

ME: I appreciate that. Thank you.

HIM: And now you're breaking up with me.

ME: Yes. I'm sorry.

HIM: Well it's totally fucked. What was the point?

ME: Point of what?!

HIM: Being faithful.

ME: I don't know? Perhaps it was its own reward and you now get to feel like a virtuous person. Perhaps the point is you don't have an STD. Perhaps the point is you didn't sleep with a Thai prostitute so therefore you didn't perpetuate the dreadful sex-tourist culture in that country to the detriment of its entire female population.

HIM: She was not a prostitute.

I am aware this is a pretty one-sided account because it's my version of the story and I admit I've made myself seem a lot more articulate than I am in real life, where I hardly ever speak in full and complete sentences. But one thing you have to trust me on is that she absolutely was a prostitute. I have been to that same part of Thailand he visited. I was there for a week doing some gigs, and in that time I studied the goings-on Jane Goodall-style. As a middle-aged white woman in Phuket it is very easy to move about unseen. You can eavesdrop and observe things close-up because no one notices you are watching. No one can see you. Middle-aged white ladies are invisible in Thailand. The local women can't see you because you are of no financial interest to them. The local men can't see you because you are old and huge and resemble something they would only see in a zoo or museum exhibit under a sign that says: 'Shrill Harpie. Native to The West.' And certainly the white men can't see you either because, to paraphrase Obi-Wan Kenobi, you are not the whores they are looking for.

In general I find white men in Thailand a little delusional. So often they seem convinced that they have met the one woman in the bar who is not a prostitute. This tiny, beautiful, openly adoring woman who tells them how handsome they are just happens to be the one woman in the bar who has a thing for overweight men twice her age. She is the one woman who dreams of being pawed by a large, sweaty man with fingers like raw pork sausages. How fortuitous! What are the odds?

I realise there are plenty of decent white men who go to Thailand on holiday with their wives and families but they can't see you either. That's because they don't see anything, they walk around the place looking intently at the ground, afraid to look up lest they accidentally make eye contact with a local girl who will then approach and shamelessly try to crack on to them despite the fact their wife or girlfriend is standing right next to them, holding their hand. I also realise I was in a particularly notorious part of Thailand, so to be fair, 'hashtag not all Thailand' or whatever.

When I think about my trip to Thailand I always remember the man who sat next to me on the plane on the way over. A man whose name I never learned but whom I will never forget. He was pink and sweating even before we hit the Bangkok heat. He flopped into his seat, appropriated both armrests, then turned to me (I'm not sure how he saw me, maybe the middle-age-lady vanishing cream doesn't go into effect until you hit Thai airspace) and said, 'So what takes you to Thailand? Business or pleasure?'

'Business,' I replied.

I didn't ask him why he was going because I didn't want to know. Also, I'm not a big chatter on planes and I didn't want to encourage any kind of back and forth.

Didn't matter, he was happy to tell me whether I asked or not.

'Well, I am going for Pah-lejjahhhhh.' That's how he pronounced pleasure. 'Pah-lejjjaaaahhh.' And in case the lecherousness is not coming through on the page, as he said it he also rubbed his hands together much like you would before tucking into a tasty meal. 'Pahhhlejjjahhhh'—rub rub rub.

My soon-to-be ex-boyfriend, the stoner, and I went around and around for a good two hours, neither of us able to prove our point to the other. His point being that I had no right to break up with him because he had been faithful. My point being that his point didn't make sense! And my other point, the one he absolutely would not concede, being that 'The woman was a freakin' prostitute!'

This bizarre exchange only served to strengthen my resolve and there was no way I was going to be talked into us staying together. I eventually left his place and went home, knowing I'd done the right thing breaking up with him.

About a week later he called and asked if we might have lunch together, just as friends, and I agreed. We met up and I enjoyed our friendsy lunch, it was easy for me because I wasn't looking for anything else. I was both relieved and pleased that we'd broken up, my days were no longer aggravated by nonsensical conversations or tortured by hours spent imploring him to get out of bed—things that made me feel like our relationship was more mother and errant teenage son as opposed to girlfriend and boyfriend.

The problem, I soon realised, was that he took my agreeing to have lunch with him as a sign that there might be a chance we could get back together. For reasons I can't explain, he still liked me and hoped we could resolve our differences. He called again a couple of days later and suggested we have a drink, again, just as friends. This time, I said no. Which made me feel like an arsehole. Cos after all, he just wanted to be friends, why couldn't we be friends? And the answer was, I could just be friends but he couldn't. Therefore, I needed to be an arsehole. That way he could begin the process of not liking me. And if you want to get over someone, you need to be able to not like them for a while.

One of the things that makes break-ups so difficult is the fact that no one is prepared to be the arsehole. Everyone wants to be liked, even by the person they don't want to go out with anymore. That is why people say stupid, self-serving things when they break up like, 'Please don't hate me.' You can't say that. The person you are breaking up with needs to be able to hate you, at least for a while. Also, you are breaking up with them, you are crushing their heart, destroying their happiness, at the very least you are totally ruining their day, so you do not get to ask them to do you any favours like 'not hate you'. Let them hate you. Don't answer their calls or texts because that is tantamount to giving false hope. You want them to phone a friend and vent about what an arsehole you are for not taking their calls.

I'm pretty sure it was Buddha who said, 'To bring ultimate joy to others, one must sometimes tread the less noble path and embrace the way of the arsehole.'

THE GRAVEDIGGER'S WIFE

Childless women between the ages of thirty-six and forty-three should not be allowed on internet dating websites. In fact, it would be best if they didn't date at all for those seven years because this is a very dangerous time for women. Nature makes it virtually impossible to make a sensible decision about a partner during this period.

This is the age when a woman's hormones go into overdrive and the ovaries start conducting a fire sale, they are determined to get rid of all the stock before the shop shuts down completely. That's right, all those eggs have got to go. That's why multiple births are more common in older women, because the ovaries are spruiking eggs like a late-night infomercial host.

'For a short time only, you get not one, not two, but three eggs! That's a bonus two eggs on top of your regular egg, no extra charge but you must ring now! (Qualityofeggsnotguaranteed).'

Consciously or not, women get blinded by the need to use those eggs and take advantage of such an incredible offer. Everyone knows that women love a sale. Problem is, now, instead of looking for a partner they actually like, someone they get along with, someone to whom they are attracted, someone they share similar values with, etc. etc. they start thinking like this: *Hmm, Geoff seems nice. He's solid. And he has a sensible job. He would be a good provider. I think I love him.*

No woman in her twenties sits around dreaming about meeting a man who is solid, decent and sensible. That doesn't happen until your mid-thirties when you start thinking of relationships in terms of 'near enough is good enough', 'beggars can't be choosers' and 'I guess this'll do'.

The one upside of this period in a woman's life is that she becomes a maths expert. Even those who have never shown any aptitude for mathematics in the past suddenly become the best number-crunchers in the business. For a childless woman in her mid-thirties the mental arithmetic starts on the very first date. Once they've said 'hello', the calculations begin.

'Hmm, Geoff seems nice. Solid. He would be a good provider. I think I love him. Okay, so I'm thirty-six now, social convention says we'll need to date for about twelve months before we can get married, so that will make me thirty-seven which means we'll have to start trying for a baby straight away, it might take a while, so I could be thirty-eight before I even fall pregnant. If I want my child to have a sibling I'll have to get knocked up again immediately so I can have my second child before I'm forty . . . Sorry . . . what was that, Geoff? Would I like a glass of wine? Oh yes please, thank you . . . Actually, maybe I shouldn't, I'm trying to get pregnant.'

I speak from experience. Even though I was not aware that any of this was going on in my head at the time, I now understand why, in my late thirties, I went out with an almost mute gravedigger for six months.

I was living in London and I met this man on the internet via a website called lonelygravediggers.com. I'm kidding, obviously, but I admit I was strangely intrigued by his profession, which was one of the reasons I agreed to a date. He lived in Somerset and we made plans to meet up for dinner the next time I was down that way doing gigs. He met me at the train station and we greeted each other like pigeons, heads bobbing back and forth as we tried to negotiate whether we should kiss each other on the cheek or not. I came in for a quick peck then realised he wasn't going for the kiss, so I pulled back just as he realised I *was* going for the kiss and he leaned in. Sometimes being Anglo is so difficult. It's a shame we don't have a European-style standard way of greeting one another like the French with their two kisses, one on either cheek, or even the Dutch with their three kisses, one on the right, one on the left, one on the right again. That's one too many in my opinion but at least there's never any confusion, unless of course a Dutch person greets a French person, then there might be a bit of English-style awkwardness on that last kiss.

Eventually we settled on a clumsy, half-hearted hug that turned into more of a stiff, congratulatory pat on the back as only I committed to the hug.

As we walked to his car he asked if it would be okay to make a quick detour before we went to the restaurant as he needed to drop something off at work. No problem, I said, and jumped in the car. The sun was setting, I was in a lovely part of England and that's when I panicked. I realised I was driving off to a graveyard with a complete stranger. And, not only that, I'd been too embarrassed to admit I'd met this man online so I hadn't told anyone where I was going or what I was doing. How foolish. It suddenly became very clear to me that *I* was the thing he was going to 'drop off at work'. It was so obvious, I couldn't believe I'd been so stupid, this man was going to kill me and toss me into a grave he'd prepared earlier. There was even a shovel on the back seat of the car! How could I have missed that?

As we drove through the gates of the cemetery, I imagined he'd planned things out to the very last detail. No doubt there was a funeral on tomorrow which meant he'd have dug the grave today, only instead of digging it the usual six feet deep, he went down an extra foot. He'd arranged my murder as a date so that I would get in the car willingly, there wouldn't be a struggle. He knew no one would have noticed anything abnormal about our awkward greeting because we were in

England and that's how everyone greets each other—stiffly and self-consciously. So now all he had left to do was kill me. I figured he'd probably do it by whacking me on the back of the head with that shovel I had spotted on the backseat and I'd already decided not to fight. I would just stand really still but try to remain loose and relaxed and hope he killed me with one blow. If I'm completely honest, a terrible thought crossed my mind at that moment and, for a split second, I thought I kind of wouldn't mind if he had sex with me first. But then I quickly went back to thinking about his clever plan and what he would do after he'd killed me. Aided by the cover of darkness, he'd pick up my limp body, haul it over to the pre-prepared, seven-foot grave and toss me in. Then he'd cover my body with a light scattering of topsoil and possibly a sprinkling of lime. (I think I saw that on *The Wire*, you cover the corpse with lime to prevent it decomposing and causing a stink.) And then, here was his absolute genius, tomorrow at the funeral, the bereaved would lower the coffin containing their loved one right down on top of me. No one would ever know. I'd go missing without a trace. The perfect crime.

That drive to the cemetery was probably the quietest I have ever been in my life. I don't think I spoke a word the entire trip. And I was really torn because once I'd accepted I was going to die, I wanted to make sure it was as painless as possible. I wanted to say to him, 'Hey, can you please hit me twice? Give me a second really hard blow to the back of the head, even if it looks like I'm already dead, hit me again. I want to make sure I'm really dead not just unconscious. I don't want to wake up and discover I've been buried alive. Thanks mate!'

But then nothing happened. He dropped off the shovel, got back in the car and we drove to the restaurant. I couldn't believe I had cheated death, I felt quite euphoric, I had been so sure my number was up. And perhaps it was the sheer relief of not being dead that made me think, *Hmm, this guy's nice, he didn't kill me, I can really see this working out.* More likely, however, it was because I was thirty-eight and my egg-chucking hormones were doing my thinking for me. Although, I did genuinely find the topic of gravedigging pretty interesting and I learned quite a bit. For example, sometimes they still need to dig a grave by hand if the 'plot' (*I know all the lingo*) is surrounded by headstones and they can't get the JCB (*that's a digger*) through to the site. Also, the volume of ashes produced is related to the size of your bones, not how fat you are. Turns out being big-boned is a real thing, not just something people say to rationalise obesity. But the conundrum is, you'll never know whether you're fat or big-boned until you're dead and someone is shovelling your ashes (*or 'cremains'*) out of the furnace. I suggested perhaps the crematorium should offer two sizes of urn. A large one with a plaque that says, 'See! I told you I was big-boned!' and a smaller one inscribed with the words, 'Look at that. Turns out I was just fat.'

I got a lot of insider knowledge about the dead body business that night, I can even remember what temperature the furnace needs to reach in order to burn the bodies, which is around 1400 degrees Fahrenheit. If the temperature drops too much lower than that the smell in the air around the crematorium starts to get a little bit roast chickeny apparently. And no one wants to think of their loved ones being roasted by the Colonel and served up in a bucket of KFC.

So initially there was plenty of dinner table conversation. Although if I'm honest, it was usually more like an interview than a conversation. I'd ask questions. He'd answer them. And while the cemetery/gravedigger stuff was good fodder for a few dates, once I ran out of questions, we didn't have a lot to talk about. That's when I noticed that he really only spoke when spoken to, in that he was happy to answer any of my questions but he didn't have any questions for me in return. I'm not saying I'm fascinating but being a comedian is not an entirely uninteresting job. Surely there was something he wanted to know about me. But no, apparently not. I'm not sure he even knew I was from Australia—he certainly never asked about it. Maybe he just thought I talked funny and didn't want to draw attention to it. I'd like to think that his reluctance to chat wasn't because he wasn't interested in me but rather that he just didn't like talking. At all. He could happily sit in a restaurant all night and not say a word. In fact, I think he'd have preferred it. I, on the other hand, cannot bear being that couple with nothing to talk about over dinner, especially when I'm out in public. Poor man, I think he was totally misled by my petrified silence on that first car trip. He thought he'd finally found the perfect woman.

I told myself it didn't matter. After all, I thought, there's more to a relationship than talking. When I read that sentence now it makes me laugh so hard. Talking is the very essence of a relationship. If we'd just been able to communicate, then I may have been able to come to terms with our other core differences. Like the fact that he liked his steaks well done. Really well done. I don't have proof but it wouldn't surprise me to find out he sometimes popped a steak in his 1400-degree oven at work—that's how well done he liked them.

Or that he had a whole cupboard full of tinned tuna and, when he wasn't cremating steaks, he would eat the tuna straight out of the can. I am positively phobic about tinned tuna, I cannot even open a can of it, lest a drop of that disgusting tuna juice gets on me. The stink of it makes me gag. But he loved it. Straight out of a can with a spoon. Num num.

After several quiet months together we decided to go overseas and not talk to each other there. Bit of a holiday. Give ourselves something new not to discuss over dinner.

It was tough to agree on a holiday destination. We had all of Europe on our doorstep but he wanted to go to the Caribbean. And yes, the Caribbean is lovely but I don't like the sun much. I mean, I think the sun is a topnotch source of light and heat and a brilliant thing for the earth to revolve around but I don't want to lie out in it. Especially not for a whole week. That's less of a holiday, more of an expensive way to get skin cancer. But I agreed because he said it was his favourite place and I was just thrilled he'd said anything at all. I even thought,

This could be a real game changer. We will go to his favourite place and he will be so relaxed and comfortable that he will finally open up to me . . . Hmm, he might even propose! It's funny because I was certifiable.

He didn't propose, obviously. It was highly unlikely that the first question he ever asked me would be 'Do you want to get married?' So we spent the holiday in silence. At dinner one night I seriously considered doing a bit of fake sign language. I figured I'd start flapping my hands around as if I was signing, then everyone else in the restaurant would think we were a deaf couple rather than one of those sad, ill-suited couples who have absolutely nothing to talk about.

Unbelievably, we carried on this charade of being a couple for *six months!* Thanks to nature, I was in no state to make a sensible or rational decision about a potential life partner and I admit I might also have been slightly blinded by the fact that he did look like someone who dug holes for a living. In a good way. In a way that made him the fittest person I have ever had the good fortune to be nude with.

So nature explains why I was in the relationship but what the hell was in it for him? His ovaries weren't having a closing-down sale. And I don't look like someone who digs holes for a living, I look more like someone who watches someone who digs holes for a living and then calls out, 'Hey I think you missed a bit.' Why on earth was he hanging around? Was he a masochist? Did he enjoy the pain of being around a woman who talked all the time? Did he have a thing for being badgered and bombarded with incessant questions? Was he into women who constantly served up his steak medium-rare hoping he wouldn't notice, thinking maybe he'll just try it and realise it's delicious and finally admit that a well-done steak is an abomination? It didn't make sense. Was he an idiot?

Quite the opposite, it turns out. He was very smart. I lived in a two-bedroom flat in a lovely part of London called Highgate. Though the flat was modest the locale was great and, best of all, the flat had heating. The pipes at my place never froze (it wasn't wartime after all) so I always had hot running water and a nice big bath. He, on the other hand, worked for a chain of cemeteries and lived half the time in Somerset, the other half in London. In Somerset he had a house, in London he lived on site at the cemetery. That's right, he lived at the graveyard. In a caravan. As it's virtually impossible to heat a plastic and plywood box sitting out in the open in freezing English winter temperatures, the caravan's pipes were pretty much frozen solid from October to February. And then along came me with my lah-di-dah fancy I-live-in-a-heated-flat-right-near-your-cemetery ways.

I can see how I was pretty appealing. Right up until spring came and the weather warmed up. Then enough was enough. It was one thing to tolerate a woman yammering at you endlessly in order to stay warm, but once those pipes unfroze there was no need to put up with that rubbish. He didn't say anything (no surprise there) to indicate that the relationship was over, he just stopped coming around. I wrote him a long, ridiculous email about how hurt I was (I seem to really enjoy playing the wronged female, it's quite embarrassing) and how I'd believed we had a real future together. I did. I really did. I know, it's so cringeworthy I can barely admit it. He was a little less emotional in his response and simply emailed back, 'Sorry. Regards, Alan.'

With hindsight, I actually respect him for that. I mean, exactly what kind of future was I imagining? One where I would be 'The Gravedigger's Wife'? And while that does sound like a fabulous Joanna Trollope novel, it also sounds like a tale that would be full of murder and intrigue. The only real question would be who would murder whom first?

I'd already given a lot of thought (on that first date) as to how he would get rid of me but what if I snapped before he did? How would I kill him? I've no stomach for violence or gore so I would have to use poison. I could probably sprinkle Ratsak on his overdone steak or spray Roundup into his tuna, it's not like I'd be ruining the taste of either. While killing him would be tricky, disposing of his body would be a cinch. I wouldn't bury him, I'd want to leave no trace of either him or the poison. There'd have to be a burning. This was where all my interview questions would pay off. I knew how to turn the furnace on at the crem, I even knew that you called it 'the crem'. I knew which buttons to press to open the doors and roll him in, I also knew that it was important to preheat the oven to 1400 degrees. Put that sucker in to a cold oven and suddenly everyone in the area would be tipped off to an unscheduled cremming due to the delicious smell of roast chicken and gravedigger in the air.

I LOVE A BIDET

Just after I turned forty, I found myself in a relationship with a very normal, very decent but rather handsome man. He was an engineer, which is ironic, considering everything I'd said and thought about engineers twenty years earlier when I was at UTS. I'd obviously changed my tune . . . or, more likely, it was because I was still in that dangerous seven-year period when a woman thinks every man she meets is 'solid' marriage material. We went through the motions of being a couple, and ticking off the couples 'to-do' list at speed because as forty-somethings there was no time to waste. Three months in and we were hell-bent on moving this thing forward. We'd met each other's parents, met each other's friends, discussed how one might have children this late in life (well, how *I* might have children, he already had one) and we'd even taken a mini-break together. A little romantic weekend away, staying in a quaint Bed and Breakfast run by an overly friendly couple called Lorraine and Bob.

I'm not a huge fan of B&Bs, I find the Holly Hobbie décor a little creepy and there are often so many trinkets and knick-knacks that it feels like you're sleeping in a homewares shop. I once stayed at a B&B that had price tags on everything in the room. I wasn't sure if that meant the things were for sale or if the hosts just wanted you to know how much they'd spent on lamps, candlesticks and trios of stone pears. Mostly what I don't like about B&Bs, however, is the way the hosts are always lurking around. I know it's their house, so technically they're allowed to wander about wherever they like, but it's the way they do it so quietly, like they're always hoping to catch you out doing something untoward. Like pilfering a snifter of brandy from the honesty bar or moving the knick-knacks around so the bronze naked lady lamp looks like she's got a ceramic pineapple going up her arse, or, touching up the Ye Olde Dressmaker's Dummy in the hallway by honking it on the pointy fabric bosoms. My sister did that once, it was very funny. Even funnier when we looked up and saw the owner of the B&B staring at us. Where had she come from? Honestly, she was like a human Segway that woman, silently rolling around the B&B, appearing just without warning. 'Hellooooow! Having a nice time?'

It's always a slow and laborious process checking into a B&B because the hosts like to explain everything in extreme detail. Lorraine and Bob of Peppertree House were no exception. Lorraine took us on a tour and showed us the house, the gardens and every single feature of the room we were staying in. Bob came too, although I'm not sure why, he didn't say a word the whole time. He was more like a human knick-knack—I should have checked him for a price tag. Lorraine was very much in charge of both the tour and the oversharing.

'Okay, come on and we'll show you around. This is the lounge area. It's lovely and cosy by the open fire, honesty bar over there and please help yourself to a slice of cake. Bob made that cake, didn't you Bob? He's been doing a lot of baking since we retired up here and he really loves it. That's banana rum cake, his own special recipe and he's always a bit heavy handed on the rum, so go easy! Best not to get behind the wheel after you've had a piece! (Chuckle chuckle.) We have a few other couples staying this weekend, so you might run into David and Anne, they're from Oberon, lovely people. And then we've got Michael and Paul staying in the front room—gay I think, not that we mind, everyone's welcome here, aren't they Bob? Bob's got a lesbian daughter from his previous marriage. I think he still hopes it might be a phase but I doubt it, she's quite mannish, isn't she Bob? Always wearing those big, baggy trousers, which is a shame really because she has such a lovely trim figure. Alright, now these are the stairs, have you used stairs before? Okay, good, well let's go on up and show you your room. There's two keys, the big one opens the front door downstairs, the smaller one with the blue dot, this one, opens your room. Put it in the lock, turn it to the right, like that, did you hear the click? That means it's unlocked and now you can push the handle and go in. Do you want to try it? There you go, you've got it.'

Lorraine took us through the light switches, the aircon, the tea and coffee-making facilities and the taps in the bathroom, cos 'sometimes they can be a bit fiddly'. Then I noticed there was a spa bath and knew that was going to add at least another ten minutes to the room induction. There is always an entire separate compendium of rules for spa baths and Peppertree House was no exception. Desperate to nip the spa presentation in the bud, I quickly said, 'Don't worry about it, Lorraine, we won't be using the spa.' But to no avail, Lorraine didn't believe for a moment that we wouldn't want to sit in the spa bath with a plastic flute of champagne (no glass in the spa please) and look out at the scrubby Australian landscape. One day I'll get up the courage to tell a B&B owner the real reason I won't be using the spa bath, and that's because I don't trust that it's ever been cleaned properly. To properly clean a spa bath you have to fill it and then run the jets to flush them out after each guest, that way there's no dirty, pube-filled water remaining in the pipes. I know this because I once worked as a housekeeper at a resort and that is what we were supposed to do every time we cleaned a room with a spa bath and we never did.

The mini-break itself was fairly uneventful which, considering my history of travelling with boyfriends, I took as a really good sign. While it was only a couple of days away, I thought we travelled quite well together although I may have been somewhat blinded by the fact that he carried my suitcase for me. I know that sounds terrible but I love it when a man carries my bag. I used to get all offended by that sort of thing when I was younger—'I can do it, I'm not useless!'—but now, after a lifetime of being on the road, travelling around on my own, lugging suitcases up and down stairs, on and off trains and planes, and in and out of overhead lockers and boots of taxis, I admit that I find it one of life's great pleasures to have a man carry my suitcase. Apologies to the sisterhood.

Emboldened by our mini-break success, we jumped ahead on the couples' to-do list and planned a proper holiday together. 'Proper', in this case, meant a trip to Europe. It's always tricky going to the northern hemisphere from Australia because you feel obliged to go for an overly long time in order to justify the price of the airfare. You have to include multiple countries on your itinerary to make going all that way worthwhile and you need to take a large amount of luggage to sustain you for the extended period of time you'll be away. He'd never been to Europe before so we decided to do five cities in five countries—London, Paris, Berlin, Seville and Amsterdam—in one three-week hit.

Things looked pretty good for us on paper. He didn't mind at all that I liked planning and booking ahead. Also, the internet and TripAdvisor had been invented by then, which in theory should have made organising a holiday a lot simpler. In reality, though, it just meant I wasted an awful lot of time looking at endless options and alternatives. I spent hours searching for the ultimate hotel or apartment in every city, comparing and contrasting photos of each place, reading the reviews and then doing that thing where you keep upping your price range by fifty bucks, then another fifty, then another fifty *just* to see if things might suddenly get fabulous. Then, when you suddenly come across something fabulous, you get all excited until you remember you're now three hundred bucks outside your price range and you return to the more affordable options.

It's very stressful and a lot of pressure being the person who picks the accommodation because you always feel like it's your fault if it's no good. And I guess it is.

Credit to my partner, he didn't say anything negative when we arrived at the hotel (I had chosen) in Seville, which was on the wrong side of town, looked nothing like it did in the pictures and was totally underwhelming. But sometimes silence speaks volumes and I imagined how disappointed he must have been. I'd given him the impression I was all over this internet travel booking stuff.

I was already feeling a bit defensive even before we got up to our room and found it to be creaky, cheaply furnished and, above all, really, really dark. Because it didn't have a window. Not one. You have to love the Spanish for their complete disregard for building codes and laws in general. Clearly a bribe can still get you a long way in Spain.

Bottom line was I'd chosen a total dud. I was really cranky with myself for getting it wrong so I attempted to gloss over my poor choice by playing the glad game, Pollyanna style, and finding some positives. One of which was the fact that there was a bidet.

I love a bidet. For so many reasons. First, they are a great way to shave your legs in a hurry. It's like a sink but at leg level. And no, before you ask, it is not like you're shaving your legs in a toilet. For a start, you don't put your foot *in* the bowl, you just rest it on the edge but more importantly, the bidet is *not* a toilet. The number of times I've had to explain this to people, you do not pooh or wee in the bidet. The bidet is for washing yourself *after* you've been to the toilet. And what is not to like about that?

Who doesn't want to be clean as a whistle down there?

My boyfriend and I had already had slight tension over exactly how clean he was down there based on the state of his underpants, which I was forced to see because he often stayed at my place and his underpants would end up in the laundry basket, which I really objected to. I didn't want his 'visibly soiled' undies touching my clothes in the dirty clothes basket. He couldn't see the problem because everything was going in the wash anyway so what did it matter. It mattered because the underlying problem was that I could never get my head around how your underpants could end up in that state.

We argued about it often, going around and around in circles, with him claiming I should stop examining his underpants and me countering that I couldn't avoid looking at them if they were in the laundry basket and I happened to be doing the washing that day. The argument always ended the same way, with me shouting at a grown man, 'Jesus Christ can you not just wipe your arse!' He was an engineer, for godsake, how could he not understand such simple mechanics?

Secretly, I had always believed that a bidet would be the answer to all our problems. If I had my way, they'd be standard issue in every single bathroom in Australia. So in our miserable, dark apartment in Seville where you could barely see two feet in front of you let alone see pooh on underpants, I put on my happy face and declared how exciting it was to have a bidet and urged my boyfriend to give it a go.

'Oh wow, there's a bidet! Excellent!'

There was silence, so I said it again, even more enthusiastically and with even more exclamation marks.

'A bidet! You know?! A bidet!!'

At this stage I started to suspect maybe he didn't know what a bidet was, otherwise surely he'd be as excited as me. So I explained it.

'You wash your bum in it after you've been to the toilet. Oooh and look, this one's got a special bum-gun hose. You shoot it up your asssss, makes it even easier to wash your asssss.'

I kept saying asssss like that, the American way, with a short 'a' and with multiple 'esses' to try to make the experience sound lighthearted and fun. But obviously it wasn't working because I was still getting nothing.

'Try it!' I said, by this stage brandishing the bum-gun hose, giving it a little squirt—yet another way to indicate the amazing fun-ness of it.

'No thanks,' he said.

Just like that, no interest. And let's not forget we'd been travelling for about twenty-four hours at this stage, so if ever there was a perfect time to hose out your downstairs area, this was it.

'Come on,' I said.

'No.'

'Why not?'

'I don't want to.'

'What do you mean? Just try it, won't hurt you.'

'No.'

'You won't even try it?'

'Nup.'

'Oh my god, why? Why not?'

'Because I don't want to.'

'Why don't you want to?'

As tedious as this conversation is to read, it was even more excruciating to be involved in at the time. Even now, as I'm transcribing it, I feel like we were doing some scene from *Waiting for Godot*. Only with bidets instead of park benches and actual bums instead of bums as in hobos.

And not unlike *Waiting for Godot*, it wasn't about to end quickly either. We carried on.

'Oh my god, stop going on about it.'

Frustrated by his stubbornness, I took the argument to a whole new level of stupid, 'It's not going to make you gay. Is that what you're worried about? That the water will shoot up your bumhole and make you gay?'

'What? You're not even making sense!'

He was right, I'd really lost it. And I was yelling. Once you're yelling, it's game over. You cannot win the argument by shouting. Especially when the main word you're shouting is 'bidet' and even though you are shouting it, you're still trying to maintain the accurate French pronunciation, 'bih-dayy'. I knew I was wrong, I knew I sounded like a banshee, but I wasn't giving up. I was having all sorts of irrational thoughts like *I will hold you down and hose your bum out myself if I have to*.

I didn't say that though, instead I shouted, 'Oh my god! Just use the bih-dayyy!' (Still pronouncing it all French and fancy.)

'I don't want to talk about it anymore.'

'You don't have to talk about it, you just have to wash your arse.'

It would have gone on longer but he had the good sense to walk out. That poor man. It was day one, we still had three weeks to go, and I'd booked all of our accommodation so I knew that pretty much everywhere we were staying would have a bidet.

Hard to believe that we completed the trip and even harder to believe that we stayed together for quite a few months after that. If I was him I'd have left that hotel in Seville and never come back. Obviously we never went overseas again and I addressed our continuing problem with a bit of lateral thinking. I threw out all his underpants and replaced them with black ones. Out of sight out of mind.

A SECURITY GUARD, A TYPOGRAPHER AND A PLUMBER ALL WALK INTO A BAR

The worst date of my life was only forty-one minutes long, though it felt like an eternity. Not surprisingly, it started on the internet, where all bad dates start.

I headed off to meet Jack, a lawyer, who, according to his profile, worked in international law, whatever that means. I turned up at the bar and was greeted by Jack-whose-name-turned-out-not-to-be-Jack but whose real name was Barry. For a moment I thought I'd accidently approached someone else's date, which is very easy to do these days with the amount of random, blind hook-ups that are happening every-where, courtesy of apps like Tinder and sites like RSVP and lonelygravediggers.com. Barry assured me that I hadn't made a mistake and that he was actually Jack. His real name was

Barry but his mates all called him Jack because he was a bit of a 'Jack' of all trades. Right. Well my friends all call me Chukka because at school I had a dreadful shag haircut that made me look exactly like that little half-ape/half-human character from the 1970s TV series *Land of the Lost*, but I don't go around telling people my name is Chukka.

Also, I would question whether Jack is a 'nickname'. 'Bluey' is a nickname, 'The Mooch' is a nickname, 'Horse' is a nickname. I know that last one is definitely a nickname because I once met a man called Simon but I noticed everyone called him 'Horse' and I caused a very awkward silence by asking, 'So why do they call you "Horse"?' In a bid to save me embarrassment, Simon aka Horse answered, 'Because my dad owns racehorses.' Still blithely unaware of my own stupidity, I pressed on like the fricken Queen of England making polite chitchat at a garden party, 'Oh that's nice . . . and do you ride?' That's when someone leaned over and whispered in my ear, 'Mate, his dad doesn't own racehorses, just think about it.'

To me Jack seemed more like an alias than a nickname. And I happen to think that if your real name is Barry or Alan or Gavin then that is something you need to confess up front, not after you've already used a relatively normal name like 'Jack' to lure someone into a date.

No surprise then that Jack, or as I nicknamed him, Barry Liar, Liar, Pants on Fire, wasn't a lawyer either. He was a security guard. However, he did have a substantial interest in international law and he'd travelled overseas extensively.

I considered telling him I was an architect. I mean, it's sort of true, I have an interest in houses and I have driven past a lot of buildings. By Barry Pants on Fire's standards, I could hang a shingle tomorrow and set up my own firm.

Two minutes into the date I already knew it was a waste of time, it was now a matter of limiting exactly how much time I would waste. In future, I told myself, I would always prepare an escape plan. I would organise for a friend to call me five minutes into the date and if all was going well, I could ignore the call. If not, I'd say something like:

'I'm sorry Jack . . . I mean Barry . . . I need to take this . . . It's my client. "Hi, Pamela, what's going on? Are you kidding me? 35 millimetres? I distinctly said 70 millimetres, it's on the plans! Tell him to read the bloody plans. What? Scotia cornices? Who the hell approved those? I will kill that builder!"' Then I'd hang up, tell Barry or Jack or whatever his name was that I had an architecture emergency and hightail it out of there.

But this time there was no way out. So when he said, 'What would you like to drink?' I was stuck and had to answer, 'I'd like a glass of red wine please.'

He said, 'I will have the same, so . . . methinks . . . I will . . . get us . . . a bottle!' As he said it, he made a very odd hand gesture, a kind of a flourish as if he was a magician trying to conjure the bottle out of mid-air. Once he realised nothing had magically materialised, he walked off to make said bottle appear in the more traditional way, by handing over money to the bar person.

A bottle? Was he *kidding*? I desperately clutched at his shirt tails as he walked off, grabbing them and his attention long enough to say, 'No, no, no! Just a glass please, I'm driving.'

Not sure why I was driving all of a sudden when I lived five hundred metres down the road and had walked to the bar but I needed to say something and 'You've got to be kidding, there's no way I'm staying long enough to finish a whole bottle of wine, I'd rather be dead!' seemed a bit rude.

Barry Pants on Fire brought back the drinks and I passed the longest forty-one minutes of my life while he told me all about his work as a security guard. Once we'd exhausted that topic, we moved on to talking about his six-year-old daughter called Ballerina or Serendipity, I can't remember exactly, maybe it was Sesquentina or Ballendipity? It doesn't really matter, knowing Barry's fondness for making stuff up, her real name was probably Margaret.

It is often assumed that I don't like children because I don't have any. This is not true. A lot of my friends have kids and I really like a lot of those kids. Not all of them but a lot of them. My sister has three and I like all of hers, my brother has a good one too. So when this guy started talking about his daughter, the problem wasn't that I don't like children, rather it was that I have zero interest in hearing about a child I have never met, who may or may not be called something ridiculous like Seranboppity and whose father I have no intention of ever seeing again. I could not have been less interested. I was bored to the point that I started thinking about dropping my wine glass on the floor just to create a distraction and momentarily halt his monologue. He clearly didn't understand the concept of 'turn-take' in a conversation. It's not difficult, it's just, 'You talk for a bit, now I talk for a bit, your turn, my turn.' Simple and yet it's surprising how many people don't grasp it. To be fair, I throw turn-taking out the window once I've had a few drinks. I'll talk and talk and tell the same story again and again when I'm drunk, but sober, I'm all about the turn-take. Jack-Barry showed no sign of giving up the talking stick anytime soon and while his words held no interest for me, I was slightly fascinated by his wide range of bizarre hand gestures. He punctuated every sentence with actions that were better suited to a flamenco dancer or flamboyant Italian waiter.

He took a brief pause in his TED talk, or whatever it was he was delivering at me, when he noticed my glass was almost empty.

'Another red for you, madame?' he said, rolling the 'r' on 'rrred' and Frenching it up with his 'madame'. Seriously, who was this guy? I was ready with my excuse this time. It should have been a great one, considering I'd had forty-one whole minutes to come up with it but he'd numbed my synapses and the best I could do was blurt out, 'No, no thank you, I have to go because I have to leave.' It was no faux architecture crisis but it did get me out of there. He offered to 'escort madame' to her car but again, I said, 'No thank you' because of course that would mean him walking me home to where my car was sitting in the garage. In my mind, he farewelled me by doing a half bow and doffing an imaginary cap, and he may well have, only I didn't see it because I was already running down the street, desperate to escape before another minute of my life was wasted.

For reasons I can't explain, I returned to the internet and had another crack at finding the perfect man. Surprisingly, he wasn't available online so I settled for someone who wrote a mildly amusing profile.

Things got off to a rocky start when I arrived for our date at 7.01 p.m. and he greeted me with, 'You're late.' I looked at my watch and thought he was attempting a mildly amusing joke so I laughed politely, 'Yes, sorry about that, I am indeed one minute late.'

'No, you are one hour and one minute late, we said six o'clock.'

Six o'clock? An hour late? I was so confused. Not only because I was sure we'd said seven but mostly because he was still sitting there. If someone was an hour late to meet me, I'd never know about it because I'd have left about forty-five minutes before they arrived. Who waits for an hour? He did and I don't think it was because he was desperate to meet me but rather because he really enjoyed berating people for being late.

'It's incredibly rude to leave someone waiting for an hour, I have things to do you know.' Clearly that wasn't true, or he'd have left already, but he was right, it was rude to leave him waiting. In my defence, I hadn't done it on purpose. I thought we'd said seven. (Turns out we had said seven, I checked my emails later.) I offered to get us a drink, thinking that might go some way to appeasing him and he said, 'Sure, I'll wait here, like I have been for the last hour already.' It crossed my mind to say, 'Alrighty, be back in a sec!' and then just go home but I felt guilty about being late so I got the drinks and returned. As per his request I bought him a glass of pinot noir although he wasn't too happy about it because I got the wrong one. There were two on the list and I chose the one from a region he didn't rate much. Tasted fine to me but by that stage I'd have cheerfully drunk metho to help take the edge off. His rant about pinot noir over, he moved on to the topic of fonts and finally cheered up a bit. He loved fonts. He was incredibly passionate about fonts. Who knew it was possible to get excited about Times New Roman and Zapf Dingbats? He was a font-maker by trade (a typographer maybe?) and he thought fonts were hugely important, which I found quite funny which in turn enraged him. Which in turn I found even more amusing. I already knew this date was going nowhere, not just because he got so angry about absolutely everything, from my being late, to the wine, to the fact that I wouldn't take fonts seriously, but also because he had a tattoo. Some people love tattoos, some people don't care one way or the other, and then there's me. I like skin to be clean and free of drawings. These days, it's a rare and exciting moment to find a man without a tattoo. Often they look tatt-free on the outside but then you discover there's some dirty old 'ink' lurking under a sleeve or a sock.

His tattoo was fairly innocuous, just two words inscribed on the inside of his wrist. I don't recall the exact words, it was the name of a font he'd invented, apparently, something like Chumba Sans. And of course, the tattoo itself was done in Chumba Sans. I'm not an expert on fonts, obviously, but if I had to try to describe Chumba Sans, I'd say it was 'shouty'.

There is nothing wrong with tattoos, my problem is that I am in awe of people who have them. I'm blown away by their confidence. How on earth does anyone have the balls to choose a design that they will wear for the rest of their life? I find it hard enough to choose a shade of white to paint my walls. And that's a pretty inconsequential choice. If you get it wrong, you just paint over it, in fact you probably don't even bother doing that, you just learn to live with it because how wrong can the wrong white be, it's still white and who the hell (apart from a white wanker like me) is going to notice? I loathe white wankers, people who can tell you that Magnolia is a little softer than Caucasian Whisper yet not quite as creamy as Albino Infusion, which has a bit of a pink tinge.

Banging on about the difficulty of choosing the right shade of white is the only time I would accept someone mocking me with that highly overused and clichéd pronouncement: 'First world problem!' Ordinarily I can't bear that expression. After all, we live in the first world, so what other sorts of problems are we going to have? It's unlikely I will ever be starving or living under the regime of a vicious military junta, but there are still plenty of annoying things about the first world, one of which seems to be that we're no longer allowed to complain about anything.

My point is, there's no painting over a tattoo if you get it wrong. You pick it, you're stuck with it. My god, it's like choosing one item of clothing and saying, I believe this fashion is going to endure till the day I die and this is what I am going to wear forever, every day, I will never ever tire of it. I have been through many different phases in my life. I am not the same person now that I was five years ago, let alone three decades ago. I often think about how many bad choices I could have made with a tattoo over the years. I was twenty once. I was a vegetarian once. I tie-dyed everything I owned and made my own deodorant once. (Didn't work by the way, the tie-dying or the deodorant, and apologies to those I offended with my putrid smell and revolting, cack-coloured clothing while I was in that phase.) I'm just eternally grateful I didn't get a tattoo at that time or I could so easily be stuck with a tattoo of a blurry rainbow arching over a dolphin—a dolphin that has spread with age and morphed into something that now looks more like a dugong. Or worse, I could be sporting the Chinese symbol for vegetarian dumpling on my no-longer-youthful-or-muscular upper arm. Actually there's no way I would ever have that last one but only because I'm pretty sure the word vegetarian dumpling doesn't exist in Mandarin or Cantonese. I know that because I was at yum cha once and when I pointed at a trolley of dumplings and asked if they were vegetarian, the waitress nodded emphatically and said, 'Yeah, yeah, begetarian but wih pork for flayva.' Brilliant answer. She wasn't even being funny. Note, I'm not sure if it's racist to do accents in written accounts but I am well aware that I could not say it aloud the way she said it, which is a shame because when it's barked in an aggressive Chinese accent, you really get the subtext, which is: 'Sure, whatever you want to tell yourself lady, just eat the fucking dumplings, you know they're delicious.'

The real problem with tattoos is that if you have one, I will bore you senseless with my multitude of questions. I can't *not* quiz you about your tattoo. I'm so intrigued, I need to ask you things like:

'But, what if you get sick of it?'

'Does it still mean something to you?'

'Do you ever regret it?'

'Do you think you *might* ever regret it at some point in the future?'

'What if you do start to regret it? What will you do then?'

I'm like a dog with a bone especially if someone has one of those tribal tattoos.

'So what tribe is that from?'

'When did you become a member?'

'Can you be in the tribe without the tattoo?'

'Can you have the tattoo but not be in the tribe?'

'If I got the same tattoo would I be in the tribe?'

'Is your tribe currently warring with any other tribe?'

'Do you know if there's a tribe that doesn't have a tattoo that I might be able to join?'

No matter what the tattoo, I will have endless questions. And if you have your kid's name 'inked' on you, I'll be drilling down all day.

'Really? Is that your kid's name?'

'How come you have it tattooed on you?'

'Is it because you have trouble remembering it?'

'Is it to remind you how to spell it?'

'Shahmaysne, that's pretty, I love the silent "s", did you come up with that?'

'Kammembair? Is that a boy or a girl?'

'Do you have any other children with cheese-inspired names?'

Full disclosure, I have never actually met anyone with a child called Kammembair but I figure it can't be long. There are already plenty of 'Bries' out there, so why not a 'Roquefort'—that's a pretty solid boy's name. Or maybe Cheddar. That could work. I can see some American college football star being called Cheddar. 'Coming out on to the field now, starting quarterback for the Denver Devils, let's hear it for Ched Whipslade!'

And again, I reiterate, if you have a tattoo, no judgement, good for you, I admire your confidence and the belief you have in yourself, I just don't want to go out with you for your own sake, I don't want you to suffer my exhaustive questioning. As for the man who invented Chumba Sans, I never saw him or his angry looking font again.

My last internet date before I swore off the concept completely was with a man who said he was a tradie. I'm all for tradies. Nothing better than a man who knows what he's doing around the house and can fix stuff. Very sexy. Despite my online prodding, however, he would not disclose what sort of tradie he was. I was secretly hoping for a carpenter or, even better, a cabinet-maker. Although I doubted he was a cabinet-maker, surely then he wouldn't have called himself a tradie but rather a master craftsman. I think cabinet-makers are gods and if I ever had the good fortune to go out with one I would happily trade sexual favours for cabinet-making lessons.

I turned up to the bar—same one as always—I'm so lazy, if they won't suggest a place to meet up then they get punished by having to come to my part of town. I saw an electrician's van outside and thought, *Excellent, a sparky!* I have a friend who's married to an electrician and I'm always envious of the fact that she can walk around her house and shout, 'Dave! I need a power point on this wall. Now!'

My mystery tradie was a pleasant man with a pleasant face and easy to talk to. Seems to come with tradie territory, they're always good at the chitchat. He was, however, still skirting around the issue of what his trade actually was. I asked if that was his van out the front and he said no, his truck was around the back. Eventually he told me he was a plumber. This was quite the dilemma because I have always maintained I could never go out with a plumber due to an incident that occurred many years ago. At the time, I was living in a second-floor apartment, the toilet was blocked and no amount of me stabbing at it with a straightened-out coathanger would unblock it, so I called in a toilet professional, or plumber as they're more commonly known. The plumber did his own bit of much more highly skilled stabbing work, identified the problem and then went outside to investigate the pipe that ran down the wall of the building.

I'm not entirely sure what the plumber did after that but it must have involved removing some sort of cap so he could access the blockage or something. All I know is that what happened next can never be unseen. A huge wodge of two weeks' worth of toilet paper, tampons* and, let's not be coy about it, my pooh, shot out of the pipe, splattering all over the ground and the nearby fence and the nearby plumber. The poor man was standing there covered in my pooh. And he didn't even seem phased by it. Part of the job I guess.

---

* This was back in the day when you were 'allowed' to flush tampons, you were never supposed to flush pads but apparently tampons were totally flushable. Turns out they're totally not. So if you are still flushing tampons, please totally stop, for the sake of the plumbers.

And good on him. But that's when I realised I could never go out with a plumber. How could I possibly get into bed with a man who might still have a stranger's pooh under his finger-nails or stuck in his hair? I thought about surfers and how they often have an outside shower in their backyard. If I was married to a plumber, I would need to have a disinfectant bath full of bleach and Dettol in the backyard so he could completely sterilise himself before entering the house.

And now here I was faced with my worst nightmare. A very nice man, good chatter, good looking, seemed very clean on the surface but all I could think was that at some stage, probably at many stages in fact, he'd been covered in pooh. We went out a few times but my heart was never in it, I could never get over the pooh thing. It was also slightly disappointing that he wasn't particularly handy around the house. A tradie who is no good with tools. That's annoying. I thought tradies and tools went together like cheese and gherkins.

I don't mind if someone isn't handy, an awful lot of men aren't handy. The problem is when they *think* they're handy. And this guy really rated himself as a DIY master. I still have several holes in my wall where he made multiple mistakes putting up a shelf, I have a broken tile in the bathroom that he shattered with more of his cavalier drilling work and he also broke a couple of bolts on a door when he forced them into holes that were too small. Honestly, though, while I say that the second-rate handyman stuff bothered me, mostly it was just the pooh thing.

PART FOUR

PUT LESS ON YOUR FORK,
DON'T PARK ACROSS
DRIVEWAYS AND OTHER
THINGS I HAVE LEARNED

BLACK SOFAS AND PINK LADIES

I know two things about men. The first is that if men didn't exist, if we lived in a Wonder Woman-style, ladies-only, island utopia, then there would be no black leather lounges. The world would be free of hulking, great, dark sofas that occupy more space than is reasonable.

Women do not buy these types of couches. Only men do. Go to any single man's house and you will see it—a big, black leather sofa dominating the living space. Sometimes you get a massive, aircraft-carrier-sized ottoman too. If the man is recently divorced, there's every chance he's just bought the big, black leather couch as an act of rebellion, a knee-jerk reaction to years of being forced to live with tasteful beige and taupe fabric sofas. The sort of furniture he could never relax on because he was forever worried about dropping food on it or making it dirty with his filthy feet/arse/general personage. So he celebrates his new-found freedom (often *at* Freedom) by buying what has previously been forbidden.

What a liberating time that must be for a man. To walk into a furniture shop, alone, without a woman pretending she's going to consider his opinion.

'So which one do you like, darling? Sorry? What?! That one?! Are you kidding? It's way too big for the room and in case you hadn't noticed, it's *black*! And leather! It's black leather? My god, what are we furnishing? An S&M dungeon? No way, we are *not* getting a black leather couch. Oooh, that's nice though, do you like that? Don't call it beige. It's not beige, it's stone, and it's perfect . . . Don't you think . . .? Darling?'

Instead he gets to stand in the furniture store savouring the fact that the choice is his and his alone.

'I'll take the Hulko Nero please. Yes, as a matter of fact, I did just get divorced. How did you know?'

'Lucky guess. Now, seeing as how there's no woman to stand in the way of your impeccable style choices, I wonder whether I might steer you towards this even bigger *modular* lounge instead? Available in wipe-clean faux-leather, the Ebony Colossus comes with a huge, room-swamping chaise on the left- or right-hand side. It's super comfy to lie on and watch television. Some might say it was totally size inappropriate for a small apartment (cos I'm guessing she got the house, right?) but what do *you* think?'

'I'll take it.'

The other thing I know about men is that they cannot do the grocery shopping. (Yeah, yeah, hashtag not all men. Whatever.) On paper, a man should crush the task of grocery shopping. Take a list of items, locate said items, place them in a trolley, pay, return home and collect a round of applause. I'm serious about the last bit. Women are unfairly stereotyped as being incredibly needy, whereas it's men who require a disproportionate amount of approbation for completing what can only be described as basic daily chores—things such as cooking, cleaning or taking care of one's own kids. When a man does any of those things, he expects to be celebrated as a superior human.

So even though grocery shopping seems like a fairly straightforward task, men invariably get it wrong and I blame women. You wouldn't ask someone to make you an apple pie and then hand them a recipe that says:

Make pastry. Fill with apples. Bake.
Serves 8

And yet women constantly ask men to do the grocery shopping and then hand them a list that says:

plain yoghurt
apples
potatoes
tomatoes

avocado

paper towels

toilet paper

Just like the apple pie recipe, that list is an incomplete document. Any woman who gives a man a list like that is knowingly setting him up for failure.

For a start, the term 'plain yoghurt' is very vague. What the woman actually wants is a particular brand of plain yoghurt— specifically, the one she always buys that she knows the kids will eat. It needs to have the right percentage of fat in it because yoghurt that has 2 per cent fat in it is very different to yoghurt with 10 per cent fat in it. For the record, I'll take 10 per cent every day of the week. That thin, watery 2 per cent stuff is more like milky gruel than yoghurt. The point is, none of that is mentioned on the list.

Women either need to lower their expectations and just accept what comes home in the shopping bags or raise their own standards and write more comprehensive lists. Instead of writing 'avocado', write 'avocado *open brackets* that I can use tonight to make guacamole, I don't want any of those avoca-do-shaped rocks that won't soften up for another week *close brackets*'. Admittedly, in the time it would take a woman to write out such a list, she also could have driven to the super-market, got the shopping done and returned home. So what usually happens is men get the grocery shopping 'wrong' a few times and then they're simply never asked to do it again.

It's a real shame because there are several advantages to men doing the weekly shop. Firstly, they get it done fast. They get in, they get out. They don't stop to read labels or compare sugar and salt content or dither over whether to get the cheap milk or the slightly more expensive milk that doesn't make you feel like you're killing the dairy farm industry with every sip. Also, men can carry a lot of stuff, they won't hesitate to buy four tins of tomatoes, two cans of black beans and a large four-litre tin of olive oil. As a lady with limited carrying capacity (who walks to the supermarket) I would need to spread those purchases out over several trips. And finally, men don't feel guilty about throwing in a few treats that aren't on the list. A woman might agonise for ages over buying a packet of chocolate biscuits *or* a tub of ice cream, whereas a man doesn't think twice about buying the biscuits *and* the ice cream. He doesn't care who might be looking into his trolley and judging him at the checkout.

I was pleased to see a friend of mine has adopted a softly, softly, catchee monkey approach to her husband doing the shopping. Rather than absolve him of grocery shopping duty because he's bad at it, she seems to be applying Malcolm Gladwell's 10,000-hour rule, convinced that with enough practice he'll eventually become an expert. I happened to be at their place one day when he came home with the groceries. He plonked the bags on the kitchen bench, sat down and patiently waited for his wife's assessment.

'Okay . . . let's have a look.' She dived in and started pulling items out of the bags.

'What are these?'

'Apples.'

'What sort of apples?'

'Red. You said red apples.'

'Yessss, but these are Jazz apples. The kids only eat Pink Ladies. Never mind, doesn't matter, better than last week when you got Granny Smiths. What's this?'

'Plain yoghurt.'

'It's vanilla.'

'Is it? Oh well, that's pretty plain.'

'Sure, but I can't put vanilla yoghurt on tacos.'

'Why not?'

It's a fair question. He'd probably eat them. As a matter of fact, I might too.

Next she pulled out a packet of paper towels and waved them in the air, raising an eyebrow as she did so.

'Paper towels,' he said confidently.

'Why these ones?'

'They were on special.' He looked so pleased with himself. For about half a second.

'Okay, no problem but for future reference, I don't usually get these ones because they're a bit shit and they don't absorb anything. It's like trying to wipe up with a piece of newspaper.'

'Oh.'

I thought for sure she'd snap when she saw the toilet paper he'd bought, which was a twenty-roll, bulk-buy package of the cheapest, coarsest stuff on the market. That whole family was going to be wiping their bums with sandpaper for weeks. But she didn't say a word. Clearly that was enough learning for the day. Best not to overload the pupil and crush his spirit. All in all, it was a very respectful exchange with no raised voices and no rolling of eyeballs.* I thought, *Wow, they should film this and put it on YouTube*, it was such an excellent teaching moment.

She stayed calm, he seemed eager to learn, it was all so positive. It gave me hope that in a few years' time, he might become the first man ever who is trusted to go out on his own and not bring back a big black sofa.

---

* Always be wary of rolling eyeballs in a relationship, it often signals the beginning of the end.

FOOD RULES

I recently watched a woman shovelling forkfuls of food from her plate into her mouth as she walked back from the buffet to her own table. I desperately wanted to tell her to stop. I wanted to say, *Lady, come on, we live in the first world. No one is that hungry. Your table is less than twenty feet away, just wait.* She didn't seem to comprehend that food is a delicious luxury. She acted like food was just fuel—fuel that was powering her back to her table and if she stopped stoking her engine with those scrambled eggs there was every chance she'd conk out before she got there. I couldn't bear it. I had to stop myself from yelling, 'Take your time, sit down, enjoy your food, eat properly!'

Eating properly not only means being seated but also chewing with your mouth closed. That sounds like a fairly standard directive but I've discovered, somewhat surprisingly, that closed-mouth chewing seems to be going out of fashion. All too often these days, I find myself sitting across the dinner table from someone chewing with their mouth open and showing me the whole car crash within. There is also a lot of unpleasant noise associated with open-mouth chewing. 'Smack, smack, smack,' that's all you hear, 'smack, smack, smack' as their chops flap open and shut, open and shut. That's why I have coined a new term for open-mouth chewers, I call them 'smacksmacks'.

Here's how you use it in a sentence: 'Hey, how was your date last night?'

'No good I'm afraid, he had a tattoo, but worse than that, he was a smacksmack.'

I'm hoping this word will work its way in to the vernacular along with another term my sister and I invented, which is 'chipmunking'. Chipmunking refers to the action whereby someone moves the food they are chewing into the side of their mouth so they can talk. It is so-called because the big lump of food that is now bulging in their cheek makes them look like a chipmunk. Full disclosure: I am guilty of chipmunking. I'm trying to break the habit but I come from a long line of chipmunkers. My family all love talking so much that often it's like sitting down to dinner with Chip 'n' Dale or Alvin and his singing pals, only not nearly as cute.

Another way to ensure you eat properly is to take small bites. You don't need to eat your dinner in a few giant mouthfuls, cramming it in as fast as possible, because the good news is that you don't live in a famine-stricken country or an eighteenth-century orphanage. No one is going to steal your food. Relax. Slow down. Remember, a fork is a fork not a shovel. The easiest way to tell if you have too much on your fork is if you need to turn or rotate the fork sideways in order to push the whole lot into your mouth. Eating should not require the same sort of moves you would make if you were trying to manoeuvre a couch around a corner and through a doorway. Cut it into smaller pieces and take smaller bites. Smaller bites also means less chipmunking because you'll finish each mouthful faster.

People who live alone (like me) need to be extra vigilant about their eating habits. It's hard when there's no one around at mealtimes to keep you in check, no one to sit opposite you and look horrified if you start to eat like Cookie Monster from *Sesame Street*, no one to say, 'Hey mate, that's too much!' when you make a bad judgement call and try to poke the entire dumpling or roast potato in your mouth at once and end up looking like a snake swallowing a small possum. There is a saying 'dance like nobody's watching'. When it comes to mealtimes I say, 'Eat like somebody *is* watching.'

Finally, there is the issue of smelly food. I realise I'm never going to stop people eating stinky food, nor would I want to because some stinky foods are delicious, but I do think we need a few rules. For a start, smelly food should be enjoyed either when you are on your own *or* out in wide open spaces in the great outdoors where the stink cannot get trapped and take hold and linger. What I'm saying is: enjoy your fish curry in the privacy of your own home but do not, under any circumstances, bring the leftovers into work the next day. It is a selfish and heinous act to microwave fish curry in an office kitchenette and then sit at your desk chowing down on your trout vindaloo while everyone around you is running to the windows gagging for fresh air.

Anyone trying to enter a cinema with a bag of fast food should be turned away by the usher, and if someone boards a plane with that stuff you should be able to call the air marshal and have them forcibly removed from the flight. I don't know if we have air marshals in this country but if we don't we should definitely get some. They can wage one war on terror and another war on stink. The problem with fast food is that the smell gets worse as it cools down. You literally smell the fat congealing and it's disgusting.

My top three smelly, trigger foods are popcorn, egg sandwiches and tinned tuna. I'm not one for GM foods but I do wish scientists would use their powers for good and genetically modify tinned tuna to stink less. Egg sandwiches make the list because they are doubly offensive, stinking at the time of consumption and then again ten minutes later when the toxic egg farts begin. As for popcorn, I love eating it but only at home, not when I'm out, and definitely *not* at the movies. I cannot stand the overpowering, artificial stench of popcorn in cinemas.

On a recent stand-up tour I performed in Grafton, New South Wales, where the local cinema doubles as the venue for live shows. As we were doing our sound check in the afternoon, a strong smell of popcorn wafted into the room. It turned out the cinema staff had arrived and fired up the popcorn machine in anticipation of the evening's movie screenings. It dawned on me that popcorn would also be available to the people coming to see my show. What if my entire audience walked in with buckets of popcorn? It was going to be one giant PMZ—Popcorn Munching Zone. I imagined an auditorium full of people, all staring at me, all smacksmacking on their popcorn—and the only thing worse than the smell of popcorn is the smell of masticated popcorn.

I often get nervous before a show and my anxiety manifests itself in the form of irrational thinking and meltdowns over really stupid things. The popcorn smell was going to be one of those things.

I went to my tour manager and suggested that 'we' (meaning 'he') should go and ask the manager of the cinema if she could shut down the popcorn machine and, so as to avoid complaints, she should tell people the machine was broken, maybe put a sign on it saying 'Out of Order'. I thought this was a great idea. And my tour manager agreed. He said it was such a great idea that I could go and propose it myself because there was no way he was going to ask the manager of a cinema to turn off the popcorn machine. Was I insane? Did I have any idea what the profit margin was on popcorn? I didn't. He didn't either but he said they'd be making a lot more money from popcorn than Kitty Flanagan tickets that night and went on to suggest that if *I* wanted to make some serious money, maybe I should stop wandering about the country telling my little jokey jokes and start a popcorn franchise.

Determined to prove that it was a perfectly reasonable request, I walked out to the foyer and introduced myself to the manager. That's when I saw a whole bunch of people, all lined up, not to see my show but to see the films that were screening in the other two cinemas within the same venue. It occurred to me then that my tour manager was right. There was no way they were ever going to shut down the money maker. And more to the point, why should they? I think one of my few positive personality traits is that, with a bit of hindsight, I can always see when I've been an idiot or unreasonable or, as was the case this time, both.

The cinema manager assured me that people who came to see live shows tended not to buy popcorn. Rather they bought choc tops. (The choc top, by the way, is the perfect snack for a live show. It has to be eaten quickly, which means it's usually gone before the show even starts.)

I assumed the cinema manager was just feeding me a line to try to placate me. I was pretty sure I heard her eyes rolling up into her head as I walked back into the theatre. But it turned out she was right! During the show, hardly anyone was eating popcorn! The smell was barely noticeable. Very little popcorn was brought into the theatre, even less was consumed during the show. I was so absolutely delighted by the lack of chewed popcorn stink in the theatre that I stopped the show at one point to thank the good people of Grafton for their excellent decision making. I don't know if they generally just don't like popcorn in Grafton or if they're all super savvy with their money and refuse to pay seven dollars for something worth forty cents and I really don't care. All I know is I had such a fun show that night, it was my first time performing in Grafton and I felt like I had found my people. Like-minded, non-popcorn-eating people. Except for that one man in Row C with the giant laundry-tub-sized bucket of popcorn. Sir, I hope you enjoyed the show but for the sake of the performer and those around you, next time, won't you please get a choc top.

GETTING EGGED

A good neighbour is something to be cherished. I had a great neighbour once. She always knew what was going on in the street, she brought me herbs from her garden, collected my mail, kept an eye on my place if I was away and basically was just a very nice person. The only problem was that she loved to pop by unannounced and I could never invite her in. I felt terrible keeping her bailed up at the front door for a chat, but the alternative was having her come in and having to fabricate a story about how I'd just been burgled in order to explain the state of my house. My lie would quickly be exposed as she surveyed the mess and started asking questions about why the burglars had been cooking cupcakes and an omelette during the robbery.

These days, rather than being rude and not inviting someone in, if I'm not expecting a visitor and my house is in a state (which is probably about 90 per cent of the time) I just don't answer the door. When the doorbell rings, I freeze and sit really quietly, hoping that the person on the other side will assume I'm out and go away. Note, if you intend to employ this method, it's important to switch your phone to silent because often the person will ring to say, 'Hey, are you home? I'm outside your house!' And if they hear your phone ringing it's very hard to pretend you're not in.

Once, I pretended not to be home when the police came knocking. It wasn't a brazen attempt to avoid arrest, I just didn't realise it was the police. Mind you, even if I had, I probably wouldn't have opened the door. My flat was in total disarray, as was I. It was a sweltering Sunday evening and I was sitting in my underpants watching television.

At 7 p.m. there was a knock at the door, which was pretty alarming not just because I wasn't expecting anyone but also because I lived in a security building. Whoever was out there had got into the building without ringing my buzzer. That meant they must have tailgated another resident through the main door downstairs and now they were up on the seventh floor, standing on the other side of my door. I'm sure they could hear the television, I'm sure they knew someone was home, but there was no way I was going to open the door. I had no idea who it was.

I sat stock still and waited until I heard retreating footsteps and the sound of the lift going back down. Obviously I needed to know who would be calling around uninvited on a Sunday night, so staying low, I crept into the bedroom and poked my head up just enough to look out the window and watch who walked out of the building. When I saw it was cops I near peed my pants. Why would the police be knocking on my door? Was I in trouble? Was I a suspect? A suspect of what I had no idea. I just feel instantly guilty in the face of authority. I do not understand today's youth and the way they have no fear of authority figures. I could never backchat my mum or even a frail old nun at school, let alone give a policeman attitude.

Worried that I was evading arrest, albeit accidentally, I called the local police station. I wanted to turn myself in before a SWAT team arrived to kick in my door and drag me out in handcuffs and underpants in front of all my neighbours. The constable who answered the phone took my name and address and put me on hold for a moment. I sat there wishing she'd hurry up, for all I knew they were setting up a sniper on the roof opposite, in fact there was probably a red dot on my forehead even as I was speaking to Constable Monotone. Eventually she came back and said, 'Flanagan? Black Hyundai hatchback registration LPE 977? You need to go move your vehicle.' Then she hung up.

I was still not sure what I'd done but, as instructed, I got my keys, went downstairs and walked to my vehicle—or 'car' as it is more commonly known. I'd parked it a few streets away because there was some construction work being done and there were no parking spaces available near my own building.

When I turned into the street I'd parked in, I saw my car up ahead and it didn't look right. As I got closer I saw that it had been pelted with two dozen eggs—which is a lot of eggs on a small car. I was stunned. Who would do this? Youths no doubt, or goddamn backpackers—that's who you blame for everything when you live in Bondi Junction, goddamn backpackers. That's when I noticed I'd parked across the driveway to a block of flats, a block of *twelve* flats. The eggs were hard and baked on, telling me they'd been there for quite some time.

Like a member of CSI, I started working backwards to try to recall the last time I'd gone anywhere in my car. I'd pretty much been holed up in my apartment in my underpants for about two days, which meant I'd been parked across this driveway preventing twelve households full of people from driving in or out of their building for more than forty-eight hours. From the state of baked on-ness I deduced I'd only been egged about twenty-four hours ago. Clearly the residents had given me the first twenty-four hours egg-free, which was very nice of them. I imagined they'd started by leaving terse notes under the windscreen wipers. Notes with lots of capital letters and aggressive underlining.

When people leave notes on cars, they are always quite random about where they SHOUT in caps or underline something. I totally understand why, it's because you are so enraged you can't think straight.

'PLEASE DO NOT park here <u>AGAIN</u>!!!!'

'People cannot get <u>IN OR OUT</u>!!!'

'I missed my shift today BECAUSE of YOU!! <u>Thanks A LOT</u>!!!'

After about twelve hours of being parked in, things would have escalated. No more notes about missing work, no more sarcastic pleases or thank yous. By now, they'd have been apoplectic and started scrawling abuse pure and simple.

'MOVE YOUR FUCKING CAR YOU <u>SELFISH FUCKING FUCKHEAD</u>!!!'

And then I guess they decided that two dozen eggs said more than words ever could.

There is no defence for my actions, but just in case anyone is making assumptions, like, *Wow, you must have been pretty drunk to just pull up, fall out of your car and leave it parked across a driveway!* that is not what happened. It was late at night, I was looking for a parking space in an unfamiliar street. As mentioned, I'd usually park near my own building, but because of the construction work there were no spaces available. On my third or fourth lap around the neighbourhood, where parking is at a premium, I finally saw a car pulling out. I drove straight in behind it and took the spot it had just vacated. Thinking about it with the benefit of hindsight, that 'vehicle' I'd seen pull out of the parking spot might actually have been a taxi and that 'parking spot', I could see now, was most definitely the driveway where the taxi must have pulled up in order to drop someone off.

Like I said, it's not an excuse, it's an explanation. I have been parked in on occasion and it's absolutely infuriating.

I'm actually grateful all anyone did was egg my car. I wouldn't have blamed them for slashing the tyres, keying every panel, then lying in wait for me to return so they could egg my person as well as my car.

At first, I was afraid to approach my car, in case someone was watching. If that had been my driveway, I'd have organised a round-the-clock vigil, with everyone in the building rostered on to take turns keeping watch so we could catch the perpetrator. I made a couple of passes, casually strolling by the car while glancing furtively up at the apartment block. Then, only once I was sure there was no lookout, I jumped in the egg mobile and drove off like a clown looking for a circus.

It's pretty humiliating driving around in a car covered in eggs. Everyone knows you've done something wrong. They might not know exactly *what* you've done but they know you've royally pissed someone off. Keen to be rid of the damning evidence, I went straight to the carwash. As I drove in, the carwash guy sauntered over, shaking his head. He stopped at my window, looked in at me and said, 'You got egged, mate.' He said it so matter of factly, like it was no surprise, as if there'd been a recent spate of eggings in the Eastern Suburbs.

'Yeah,' I replied, 'I got egged.'

I was charged a premium for 'egg removal', which I'm pretty sure was a made-up surcharge, but what could I say? You don't get egged for no reason. If you've been egged, you are clearly in the wrong and you must pay the price.

Later, when I got home and was able to examine the car more closely, despite having had it professionally cleaned I could still see where every egg had hit. Apparently, even after only twenty-four hours, eggs can corrode the paint job on a car. I began to have serious doubts about the wisdom of eating eggs. If they can dissolve enamel paint then what on earth are they doing to the lining of our stomachs?

I got rid of that car soon after the egging incident. I was always worried someone from that apartment block would recognise it. Even if they couldn't recall the number plate, the two dozen matte splatter marks on the otherwise shiny black duco were an immediate giveaway. And the last thing I wanted was for anyone to spot me driving around and know that I was the <u>SELFISH FUCKING FUCKHEAD</u>.

SNOW WHITE–THE EARLY YEARS

One of the things you may have to navigate when dating later in life is other people's children. It's surprising how many people have them.

To any young woman of child-bearing age who is vacillating and thinking, *Should I have children? Do I really want a child? What about my career? What about my fun, interesting life?* here is my advice. Have one. Just have one child. Because if you don't you will be forever sidelined, ignored and even disparaged every time there is a conversation about parenting or children's behaviour. Having a child gives you the right to comment on how disgusting it is that kids get nits, or how appalling it is when children in strollers are playing on iPads, or how there is nothing at all draconian about teaching your child good manners. Unfortunately—and unfairly—you forfeit your right to an opinion when you are childless. You are not even allowed to roll your eyes and be annoyed by a child running around a restaurant getting under the feet of a waitress carrying hot beverages because you couldn't possibly understand what it's like to be a parent. True, but I do understand what it's like to be that waitress.

So, for your own sake, and for the right to be able to tell a child to sit down, be quiet and behave, just have one child. No need to go mad and have half a dozen, you only need one. One is easy, you can keep it in a cupboard or a drawer (at least when it's small anyway) and just pull it out when you need it to justify joining the discussion and having your say about why immunisation is important for everybody and that herd immunity is not a 'big pharma' scam.

If, somehow, you end up like me—forty-odd, single and without a child of your own—then there is every likelihood that one day you may also end up in a relationship with someone who has children. And if you do, tread carefully. The world of the step-parent is treacherous and unforgiving. Step-parenting is difficult enough when you have your own child or children to deal with as well as your partner's. You might discover you and your partner have different approaches to parenting, which leads to two different sets of rules for two different sets of kids. However, at least if you have your own children, you are in a position where you can lead by example. You can say, 'Well this is how I do it and it seems to have worked out okay' because provided your child is alive and well, who can argue with you? When you don't have kids, you'll always be viewed as the inexperienced rookie, your only role is that of an observer who must watch and learn and see how things are done. Any of your own notions or suggestions about parenting will be dismissed as fanciful and unrealistic.

One of the first things you have to deal with as a step-parent is what to call yourself. And the answer is anything but step-parent.

There is an old adage that says it takes a village to raise a child. So based on that, I would like to suggest a new term, 'Villager'. In future if someone asks, 'Are you the stepmum?' you can answer, 'Oh lord no, I'm just the "Villager".'

If the child in question wants to know what they should call you, then you can acknowledge what a foolhardy venture it is to try to parent someone else's child and suggest they call you the Village Idiot or V.I. for short.

Call yourself whatever you like but avoid the label 'step-mother' at all costs. Thanks to fairytales, the term is laden with negative connotations and the most common word associated with stepmother is 'wicked'.

It's curious that stepfathers never get a mention in fairy-tales. I guess it's because back then, in fairytale days, no one would ever have dreamt of marrying a woman who'd already had kids. Talk about damaged goods.

Having been in several relationships where I found myself in the role of 'Villager' (albeit briefly) I have come to really resent the way stepmothers are portrayed in storybooks and movies. Invariably the stepmother is a nasty, horrible old hag who cares not a jot for the children. And she is always (yawn) wicked. But why? Why is there never a lovely stepmother? My theory is it's because all the stories pick up a long way in, once the stepmother has been at it for quite a few years. We never see the beginning of the journey, when the stepmother arrives full of good intentions. No fairytale starts with Dad bringing home his new girlfriend, and allowing us to see her do her best to fit in and find her place within the new family. We never see her navigating that tricky period where she's treading a fine line of trying not to rock the boat but still setting a few boundaries so the kids don't think they can walk all over her.

There are plenty of parents these days who are speaking out about the problem of gender balance in fairytales and how important it is for their daughters to read stories where girls are the protagonists and do more than just waft around being pink and princessy, waiting for a prince to kiss them. Similarly, I have decided to speak out about the negative stereotyping of stepmothers. I want to see the stepmum given an image overhaul and presented as a far more complex individual, not just some evil, barren old bag who hates kids.

To that end, I am currently working on a prequel to *Snow White* covering those crucial first few years after Snow White's mother died. Snow White is still a young child and hasn't yet started hanging out with woodland creatures and unusually small men with beards who work in mines, and the new queen, the soon-to-be stepmother, has only just arrived on the scene.

SNOW WHITE

EPISODE I: THE PHANTOM MENACE

It had been a tough few years for Glenn White, not only had he been grieving for his dead wife and trying to bring up his daughter Snow (who was quite a handful) on his own, he was also exhausted from constantly fending off an extraordinary number of predatory women. Turns out nothing gets a lady's hormones racing quite like a widower. And Glenn was no ordinary widower for he was also the king. So the women were in a frenzy, with all the single village ladies (and some of the married ones too) in hot pursuit. Poor Glenn could barely ride down the street in his gold carriage without women hurling themselves in front of it.

The women pursing Glenn fell into three categories. First, there were the nourishers—women who kept popping over to the castle with a lasagne or a casserole, determined to help His Royal Highness eat through the pain. Second, there were the needy-damsel types, constantly calling up to see if the king might be available to come over and help them hang a painting or thatch a hole in their roof. And third, there were the blatant temptresses. These were the really overt women who would throw themselves and their bare vaginas at His Majesty. 'Bare' meaning uncovered, as in without pants on, not hairless. Fortunately for the ladies of the time, Brazilian waxing hadn't been invented yet.

The practice of throwing oneself at a widower is centuries old but remains common today. I know of one modern-day widower who was besieged by women mere months after his wife's death, all of them desperate to fill the void left by his dearly beloved and newly departed wife. One woman was so keen she invited the widower for coffee and actually did show up without her pants on, giving him a good old Sharon Stoning under the table when he bent down to pick up the fork she'd intentionally dropped. Another turned up at his house in a fur coat wearing nothing underneath. She let the coat fall to the floor and said, 'You can have me any way you want me.' Awfully clichéd but a true story nonetheless.

Back in our land far far away, after dodging the advances of literally hundreds of women, Glenn finally announced that he would be marrying Kimberley—a sweet, young (slightly too young as far as all the thirty-something women in the village were concerned) gentlewoman from a neighbouring kingdom. A rumour went around that Kimberley had tricked King Glenn into marriage by saying she was pregnant— a pregnancy that mysteriously disappeared once she had a ring on her finger. The king dismissed this rumour as idle gossip but often wondered at the source of it. Probably one of those holier-than-thou nourisher types.

Kimberley tried her best to win over the little girl but Snowy wasn't having a bar of this new interloper. For her entire five years she'd had daddy all to herself and that's how she liked it and that's how she wanted to keep it.

Every time Kimberley made dinner, Snow White would screw up her nose and push the bowl away, saying, 'Mep. I don't like it.' Every time Kimberley suggested a game, Snow White would roll her eyes and say, 'That sounds like a dumb game for babies.'

Glenn occasionally attempted to discipline his darling Snowy but for the most part he let her behave as she pleased. Snow White's mother had died during childbirth and he felt guilty. She'd been denied a mother and he wasn't prepared to deny her anything else.

One night Kimberley made venison pie from scratch, it was quite the labour of love. Snow White took one look at it and declared it disgusting. Glenn tried to coax his cute little munchkin into eating it.

'Oh come on, Snowy my love, just try it, you might like it.'

'No. I won't.'

'How do you know if you haven't tried it?'

'Because it's yuk. And. I. Don't. Like. It!!' Snow White crossed her arms and set her mouth in a most unpleasant pout.

Poor Glenn was torn between keeping his daughter happy and trying not to upset his new bride.

'Sorry about this dear . . .' he said.

'Oh, that's okay,' Kimberley trilled, 'I don't mind. I probably didn't like venison pie when I was a child either!'

'Can I have some ice cream, Daddy?'

'No, Snowy darling, you haven't eaten your dinner,' the king said gently.

'But I hayyyte this dinner, I want ice cream.'

'Just have a few bites of Kimberley's delicious deer—'

Glenn didn't get to finish his sentence. Snow White screeched over the top of him, 'It's not delicious! Everybody stop saying that! It's disgusting, I want ice cream!'

And, as always, Glenn threw in the towel.

'Hey, hey, no screaming my love. Alright, alright, I'll get you some ice cream.'

The king shrugged apologetically at Kimberley, giving her an 'Oh well, what can you do?' look and went to fetch the ice cream. Snow White shot Kimberley a look that said, 'Take your deer pie and shove it, lady' and then snapped her face into a big sweet smile as Daddy returned with the ice cream.

Snow White beamed at Daddy and smirked at Kimberley as she shovelled the ice cream into her perfect little mouth.

Kimberley decided to try a little firm but fair discipline when Snow White asked for seconds. 'I think that's probably enough ice cream, Snow White.'

And in return Snow White howled, 'You are not the boss of me. You are not my mum, I hate you. Daddy! Daddy! Why can't I have more ice cream? You (sob) always (sob) let me (sob) have more ice cream! (sob sob sob). Daddy (sob). Daddy (sob) why are you being so (sob sob sob) mean?'

Snow White's words became unintelligible as she worked

herself into a total bate, screaming and stomping, throwing herself onto the floor and flailing around. Kimberley was appalled, she'd never seen such a display. She knew Glenn wouldn't smack Snowy (even though smacking was still perfectly legal and wouldn't be outlawed for another couple of hundred years) but surely he'd send the little minx to her room and tell her she couldn't attend tomorrow's Harvest Festival. Surely? But no. Rather, the king obeyed his little princess and dutifully fetched her some more ice cream. 'What else could I do?' he said to Kimberley. 'She gets so upset.'

Sometime later, the king carried an exhausted Snow White to bed. He read her several stories, blew out the candle and kissed her goodnight. He then returned to the parlour to enjoy a nice goblet of after-dinner mead with Kimberley.

Two minutes later Snow White appeared in the doorway, saying, 'Daddy, I'm not tired.'

'Yes you are, off you go to bed now, sweetie.'

'I need another story.'

'Alright, one more but then that's it.'

This continued all night long.

'Daddy, I'm still hungry.'

'Daddy, I need some water.'

'Daddy, I can't sleep.'

'Daddy, it's too dark in my room.'

'Daddy, there's a light coming in my window.'

And each time, with nary a cross word, the king would simply pick her up and carry her back to the bedroom, and each time Snow White would look at Kimberley over the king's shoulder and mouth the words, 'Fuck you.'

Many years later, the long-suffering Kimberley would be accused of trying to poison Snow White, though I suspect it was never her intention. In fact, I'm positive it was an accident. Kimberley probably wanted to have one night where she and Glenn could have a pleasant dinner together and enjoy a bit of grown-up conversation without his stroppy daughter interrupting to scream things like, 'I wish you were dead!' and 'You've got a stupid face that looks like pudding!' I think it's highly likely that she was just trying to knock Snow White out for a couple of hours in order to get a bit of peace and quiet.

So before we go calling any stepmother wicked, let's remember there are always two sides to every story.

COMEDIAN, HEAL THYSELF

I am mildly paranoid and anxious. Please note the word 'mildly'. I am not crippled by either of these things, I'm certainly not sitting around my house paralysed, unable to go out because I think everyone hates me. It's not nearly that extreme or interesting, it's more of a garden-variety social awkwardness that means I don't particularly like going to functions where I won't know anyone. Maybe it's because I'm not very good at starting conversations with strangers.

Here are some actual things I have said to actual people at parties in a bid to make polite chitchat.

'I like these chips.'

'Aren't these chips nice?'

'Do you have a favourite brand of hommus?'

'Oops, just broke off my chip in the dip.'

'Gee, this carpet is a bit . . .'

That last one is an example of how sometimes I just bail out on my own sentences. I can see it's going nowhere so I just give up and stop talking.

I don't know why I am like this, I mean outside of the infamous Vardy Party of '74, I've only ever had one really bad party experience. It happened soon after I joined the cast of the sketch show *Full Frontal*, a spin off from the hugely successful *Fast Forward*, a show I absolutely adored. There was a network launch at Channel 7 in Sydney. I was the only cast member still based in Sydney so I went along to the party by myself. I was new to the TV industry and, if I'm honest, I had landed my dream job way too easily. A producer had watched me do a ten-minute set at a small comedy club in Sydney and then offered me (and Julia Morris) a job. Seriously, that was it. One ten-minute audition where I just did my regular stand-up set. I didn't have to do any acting of any kind, I didn't have to produce any writing samples, and best of all, I didn't have to get all nervous beforehand because I didn't even know the producer was there. I think the word for that sort of thing these days is 'blessed', back then it was 'arsey'.

I arrived at the party and was handed a glass of champagne that was totally free. I couldn't believe it. There were glamorous TV people everywhere and even though I was really nervous about being there on my own, I also thought, *Wow if I play my cards right, not only might I be able to score a second glass of this free champagne, I might even end up meeting some actors off the telly!* I stood there looking around, thinking how great it was to get free champagne, then I decided to do something very bold and completely out of character and introduce myself to a group of my 'network stablemates'. This was something I had never done before and have never done since.

I walked up and stood at the edge of a small circle of people, leaned in (like one of those drinking birds) and said 'Hello, I'm Kitty,' in response to which a young woman, who I'm very pleased to say has never worked in the television industry since, looked at me and said, 'Don't you have any friends?' before turning back to her gang and closing up the circle. Maybe she was trying to be funny, maybe it was a joke and if I'd hung around two seconds longer she'd have turned around again and said, 'Hey, I'm kidding stablemate, get in here!' But I'll never know because I was already making a hasty exit, dumping my half-finished free champagne back on the waiter's drinks tray as I scurried out the door.

That incident goes part of the way to explaining why I prefer to avoid TV-industry events. Another reason is that I feel like a monkey in a dress when I put on fancy 'evening wear'. The main problem, however, is that my nerves get much worse around 'famous' people—not all famous people, just the ones I really admire. I think the expression 'never meet your heroes' pertains to the disappointment you will feel if they don't live up to your lofty expectations. For me it's the opposite; I don't want to say something dumb and have my hero walk away thinking, *Well she's an idiot.*

Like the time I met Lisa Wilkinson in the hallways of the ABC studios, and she extended her hand in greeting and, like a totally normal person, said, 'Hello Kitty, it's so lovely to meet you.'

To which I replied, 'Yes, yes, hello, you're welcome. Good thank you.'

Except for 'hello', none of those words make any sense. I was just taking a stab at greeting words. It was an exchange you'd be more likely to hear in a beginners' English class. Fortunately, Lisa was on her way to the Ladies so she didn't stop and try to make sense of what I'd said, she just kept moving. Meanwhile I stood there and mumbled to myself, 'Toyylet, she is going to the toilet' because sometimes, when I'm nervous, I just say what I see.

Then there was the time I saw Karen Martini on a plane. I have several of her cookbooks and I think they are fabulous, they contain recipes I have cooked again and again. I spent the entire flight glancing across at her, obsessing about how desperately I needed to tell her that I loved her cookbooks, I mean *really* love them. And not just me, my sister, my dad, my mum, we all love Karen Martini's cookbooks. In my mind, it was imperative she be told how much people adored her cookbooks (just in case the million-plus sales she'd turned over hadn't given her an inkling). As we were disembarking I pushed past a few other passengers and sidled up to Ms Martini, like a prisoner in the 'yard' about to shiv someone, and blurted out, 'I have your cookbook, it's really dirty because I use it so much.' Then my voice broke and I got all overcome with emotion and, half crying, literally choking back a sob, I added, 'I just really love it.' She was gracious and said 'Thank you' but she also looked slightly alarmed, which was totally understandable considering we were in a confined space, there was nowhere to run and a 'crazy-lady-with-a-boxcutter' vibe was coming off me in waves.

I've gone over that episode in my head many times and have come to the conclusion that my 'condition' gets worse the more time I have to think about what I am going to say. I walked past Julia Gillard at an airport once. She had her head down and was moving at a cracking pace. With no time to think about it or get weird, I simply called out 'I love you' as she sped past me. In retrospect that probably was a bit weird but I was happy with it. And it was certainly preferable to what I did years later when I ran into her at the ABC's Southbank studios in Melbourne.

I was walking towards the lifts when I saw that none other than Julia Gillard herself was standing by the lift bank. I started to sweat immediately and my brain went into overdrive.

I need to point out that I am a genuine Gillard fan. In fact my Kennedy moment, that time you will never forget where you were when it happened, was the day she got ousted. I was on tour with my sister and we were in Bendigo. It was unusual because it was a 'travel day', which meant we had a night off, so three of us, my sister, the tour manager and I, sat in my hotel room and watched those shameful proceedings in Canberra unfold on live television. I was so naïve, I hadn't believed they would actually do it. I'd even bought a bottle of champagne to celebrate when Gillard was reinstated with the full backing of the Labor party. Full disclosure, I'd also bought a bottle of champagne because it was my night off and I quite like champagne.

All of that was running through my head as I was walking towards her at the lifts. I had so much to say plus I wanted to remind her about the time we'd worked together on *The Project*. It was certainly one of my career highlights. She was prime minister at the time and was on the panel in the studio in Melbourne. I was up in Sydney in the little booth I did my live cross from every Tuesday. The director spoke to me via my earpiece telling me I was up next and that Prime Minister Gillard would be doing my introduction. I was thrilled, she'd been on the desk all night and had come across as natural, friendly and good humoured. The very opposite of how the media liked to portray her. She threw to my segment in a warm and collegiate way and when I watched it back later I saw that she had also smiled and looked amused throughout, which was very generous of her. I was like Sally Field at the Oscars, thinking—*You like me, you really like me!*

The reality of the situation was this: we weren't in the studio together, we weren't even in the same state, there's also every chance she couldn't see me—she could hear me but she couldn't necessarily see me. That's what people (including myself) often forget when they watch satellite-cross interviews on television. The screens are positioned so that, to the viewer at home, it looks like the two people are chatting directly to one another, face to face. I confess that's how I'd always thought it was done, you sat in front of a big screen with the other person on it and you talked directly to them, like a giant version of Skype. I hadn't factored in the television cameras.

It was quite a shock when I did my first ever live studio cross on *The Project* and realised I wasn't talking to a screen that had Carrie, Dave and Charlie on it, rather, I was talking to a massive camera. The only way I could see them was if I looked off to the side and watched them on a monitor. You see the 'looking off' thing a lot when kids are interviewed via satellite, they keep looking away to the monitor where they can actually see themselves and the person they are talking to.

Whether or not the prime minister had a monitor that night is moot, the relevant thing is that she was the prime minister and no doubt had a few other slightly more important things going on in her life that day. So it is entirely possible that introducing a two-bit comedian she'd never heard of, that she may or may not have been able to see, probably wasn't the highlight of her day, like it was mine. But I didn't think about any of that as I approached the lifts, I just thought it was great that we were finally going to rekindle our friendship and talk about the good times we'd had that night. I got to the lift and pressed the button, Ms Gillard nodded at me and gave me a polite hello but not before I'd already started talking at her, a bit too keen to remind her that we were old friends. 'Hello, we've met before doing a . . . um' and then I totally forgot what you call it when you do a 'live cross' so I started making this strange gesture, like someone who is trying to clap but doesn't know how to do it and keeps missing. I was crossing my hands over back and forth in front of myself trying to indicate 'live cross'. I can't believe she didn't know what I meant.

Luckily the lift arrived and thank god she was going down and I was going up. I was still doing my stupid hand thing as she stepped into the lift. That's when the words finally came to me and I shouted, 'Live cross! Do you remember?' just as the lift doors closed. 'Do you remember?' That's the bit that is going to haunt me for the rest of my days. 'Do you remember?' Yes, I'm sure it's right up there at Number 4899 of her 5000 most memorable moments.

I went to a therapist once and asked her why she thought I was like this and she said it made no sense, especially considering what I do for a living, she couldn't explain it. That was money well spent. These days I prefer to self-diagnose and have come up with my own theory, which is: I reckon I use up all my confidence on stage so I have none left for real life. It's not a great theory, but the bottom line is, it's not really that big a deal. Lots of people are socially awkward, lots of people get anxious about talking to strangers, so I should just shut up and stop worrying about it so much.

THE CIRCLE OF LIFE

An 'old' lady once told me that old is ten years older than you are now. She was seventy, so that meant 'old' was eighty. I didn't quite understand what she meant then but now I understand exactly. When I was twenty-three and working as the receptionist in a very small advertising agency, there was a woman named Sue who was incredibly chic and glamorous. She was also great at her job, the very picture of a modern, working gal. She was thirty-three and unmarried and had no children, she went on dates and had boyfriends. I wanted to be just like her because she had this fabulous life that included all those things I just mentioned and more. She had a cracking income, she lived *by herself* in an apartment that she *owned* and on top of all that she had glorious, dead-straight, shiny, dark-brown hair well before hair straighteners were standard issue in most women's bathrooms.

So I idolised Sue, but at the same time I thought she was *so* old! Thirty-three? It was a miracle she was still alive and managing to live such a full life. I simply couldn't imagine I would ever get to the wizened old age of thirty-three and still be unmarried and childless. Thirty-three?! *Jesus Christ, Sue*, I thought, *what have you been doing with* all *those years?* In fact, Jesus Christ himself chucked it all in at thirty-three. I couldn't even fathom the number. I tried to think about what my life would be like when I *eventually* turned thirty-three and I couldn't do it. It wasn't possible to imagine myself ever being *that* old. This might be why it's so hard to impress upon teens and twenty-somethings the health hazards of things like smoking and sunbaking. I remember my mum saying to me, when I was a teenager, 'Don't bake yourself in the sun or you'll be all old and wrinkly by the time you're forty.'

Oh how I would laugh at her. By the time I'm forty? So what? Who cares? Who cares what I'd look like when I was forty? Life's pretty much over by then, Mum, so thanks for the tip but seeing as how no one will be looking at forty-year-old me, then hey, I may as well be tanned and terrific in my twenties.

I should point out that, much like hair straighteners, skin cancer hadn't quite been invented yet. Slip, slop, slap had yet to hit the vernacular and the biggest anti-sunbaking deterrent was that you would end up looking like a leathery old handbag.

To be honest, though, even if my mother had said, 'Don't bake yourself stupid in the sun, you'll end up with skin cancer and die at forty' I probably would have rolled my eyes and gone 'Yeah yeah, whatev's old woman, who wants to live past forty anyway?! What on earth do you even do with your life when you're *that* old?'

Sigh. Young people are so annoying.

Now, of course, I'm part of the generation that keeps reinventing age and time. Actually, I think it's the baby boomers who started that, not Gen X. But whoever's responsible, it's clear we've moved into a new phase where people simply don't accept that they must grow old. Baby boomers, and now Gen Xers, are the classic hangers-on. They refuse to let go, and seem to believe they can fool time with their reinvented numbering system—forty is the new thirty, sixty is the new forty, etcetera. Unless of course, you're driving in a built-up area, then apparently fifty is the new sixty. When did that happen?

What I fear about getting older is not the physical degeneration, that's unavoidable. And while I'm certainly not thrilled about that aspect of ageing, I'm more concerned about the inevitable circle of life and the fact that at some point you hit the halfway point of the circle. Once that happens, you're on the road that leads back to the start. You are born, you need someone to do everything for you—feed you, change you, put up barriers to make sure you don't fall down stairs. And that's pretty much where you end up again, life comes full circle.

Along the way, as you travel the second half of the circle, there are plenty of other clear signs you are regressing and heading back to ground zero. A renewed love for salt is one sign. Young children adore salt, it's the reason you always see them licking their own snot and eating the playdough or even sucking on a metal bar (metal *is* kind of salty—metallic but salty). As you get older your taste for salt returns. And the great thing is, as a grown-up, you have access to salt in its purest form—salt—so there is no need to seek it out in snot or metal bars. It's a perfectly legal white powder that you can buy for a dollar and then dump in industrial-sized quantities on every single meal. And older people do exactly that. Salt becomes quite an obsession as one gets older. If the first words out of your mouth when you sit down at a dinner table are an agitated 'Where's the salt?!' then the bad news is you are well into the second half of the life cycle, you might even be in the final quadrant.

The other key indicator of age is craft. Craft plays a big part in your life in your early years, from doing potato prints and playing with Plasticine to making trumpets out of toilet rolls and crowding out the front of fridge with your fabulous macaroni art. And by 'art', I mean pieces of paper straining under the weight of the uncooked pasta glued to it. Magnificent works that invariably require a minimum of four magnets to hold them to the fridge.

It must be noted here that because I don't have children I have no idea whether craft is still a thing. Perhaps there's now a craft 'app' on the iPad which, while sad for kids, is a real boon for parents' fridges.

Eventually, craft creeps back into your life and that's how you know you are cruising on the trajectory towards death. I realise that sounds more ominous than it needs to, no doubt you still have a few good years left, but it's time to accept there are now fewer years ahead than behind. On the upside, rediscovering craft is joyous. Where once I thought knitted covers for coathangers were a ludicrous notion, I now think, *Oh please let there be a school fete coming up because I ache to find somewhere I can purchase knit-covered coathangers. They are so much better for your clothes!*

I learned to crochet recently as a way of passing the time on planes and have since discovered there is nothing more relaxing than wandering around a wool shop and chatting about your projects to the lovely, knowledgeable ladies who work there. (I'm talking about real, specialty wool shops here, not the likes of Spotlight, which is just not the same.) It's yet another sign of old age that I miss haberdashery shops. I never thought I would. When I was younger my mother would drag me around the haberdashery department in David Jones and I'd wonder what on earth you could ever possibly want in there besides half a metre of hat elastic to cut up and use to put your hair in pigtails, or three metres of regular elastic so you could play elastics at school. In fact, I'm pretty sure I thought haberdashery was just a fancy ye olde word for elastic. Nowadays I just like saying the word 'haberdashery' and I say it often because I'm fearful the word might disappear from the language just like the shops have disappeared from our high streets.

What I love about craft—in both halves of the circle, the youth half and the nearly dead half—is that while it is pure joy for you, it is the ultimate punishment for your family and friends because they're the ones who get given your craft. Just like when you were a kid and brought home all those pottery 'ashtrays' for your parents—'ashtray', of course, being another word for failed pot or failed vase or collapsed sculpture. Easy fix, just put a couple of dents on the edge and call it an ashtray. I was 'lucky' that both my parents smoked so I always had an outlet for my failed pottery projects. Even after my parents both quit smoking, I kept making ashtrays for them because I figured one of their smoking friends might visit. Obviously 'smoking friends' refers to the fact that the friends still smoked cigarettes not that they were 'smoking' hot. Although one of them never wore a bra and she did have quite the pair.

Now that craft is back in my life in the form of crochet, once again, it's my nearest and dearest who suffer most. Thanks to my generosity, everyone I know has a wonky beanie or a wedge-shaped scarf or a pair of fingerless gloves. (Fingers are beyond my skill level, but no matter, I'm sure all my friends are grateful for a way to keep their palms warm. Cold palms are such a common problem in this country.) The point is, even if any of these items were well made, they are hardly necessary in the near tropical Australian climate and yet everyone feels obliged to keep these itchy, shapeless, woollen tributes, rather than throw them out, simply because I made them with my own two hands.

Not everyone takes up crochet obviously. For some people craft takes the form of quilting (sticking scraps of material together) or decoupage (sticking scraps of magazines on stuff and lacquering the bejesus out of them) or scrapbooking (sticking scraps of any ol' shit in a book—fun!). Others prefer to make batches of jams and jellies and chutneys, complete with quaint, homemade labels like:

'Gwen's Gooseberry Jam'.
Ingredients: sugar, gooseberries, plus a big dollop of friendship!

Remember, so long as you make it and can gift it to unsuspecting friends and relatives, that's craft.

Men are a little bit different when it comes to rediscovering craft. Plenty of men go down the homemade chutney and relish route, some discover home brewing, and others, like my dad, start to make weapons. Specifically slingshots. Or 'shanghais' as he calls them. Even though this sounds like it would be a unique predilection, I spoke to a friend of mine and was astounded to hear that her dad, similar in age to my dad, had also taken to making his own slingshots. The only real difference was that her dad was using his to take pot shots at the teenagers next door, while mine was waging a war on native fauna.

My dad's war on fauna is exactly that. It's a war. And his enemy is the army of possums that amass (apparently) in the trees in their backyard. He takes them on single-handed, Rambo style. On a recent visit I witnessed his possum-fighting arsenal. The first thing that caught my attention was one of those super-sized pump-action water pistols. That day, the firearm in question was not operating up to its usual standard, so he had broken it down into four pieces and laid it out on the table in front of him. Like he was in 'Nam or something. He was stripping and cleaning the weapon in order to improve its performance. Apparently it wasn't shooting straight. Lest we forget, we're talking about a water pistol.

It was late evening, the sun had gone down. Satisfied he had rectified the problem, Dad reassembled his piece and once he had it fully loaded (with water) he geared up with the rest of his kit, which included a bicycle lamp strapped to his head with an old belt. This was his hands-free spotter's torch and was a necessary addition because I had refused to join the fight and act as sniper's assistant. The role of S.A. requires that you hold the torch and shine it at the enemy. Instead, I chose to be a conscientious objector. This wasn't really a problem. Dad was used to fighting alone, thus he had his bicycle light/miner's lamp headgear pre-rigged and ready to go. Most importantly, he also had his homemade slingshot sticking out of his back pocket. Meanwhile, his front pockets were full of acorn-sized seed pods that fell off a tree in the backyard. Dad was no dummy, he'd seen the potential in those seed pods some time ago and had been stockpiling them as ammo for months.

I wish I could tell you Dad burnt a bit of stick and rubbed the blackened end on his face for camouflage but a) he didn't and b) even if he had, I don't want him to sound like a nut so I probably wouldn't mention that bit. Before he went 'over the top' as it were, and into the Possum Zone (PZ) I stopped him and asked what the possums had done to annoy him so much. He said they were in the trees and if you let them hang out in the trees, the next thing you knew they'd be in your roof. In your bloody roof.

I couldn't help but think, *Yes, that is certainly where I'd take refuge, I would definitely hide in the roof if there was some mad man with a water pistol and a torch tied to his head chasing me out of the trees.*

Mostly though, I wondered why he didn't take the same approach to getting my brother to move out of the house all those years ago.

But it's really nothing to do with possums, it's simply the circle of life. My dad spent his childhood making toy weapons, crafting guns and swords from sticks and bits of timber and, from what his older brother and sister tell me, he was really good at it. And after a lifetime of jobs and seriousness and paying mortgages and supporting a family, he's found his joy in 'weapons' again.

No possums were harmed in the making of this story

because, despite what my dad might tell you, he's not that great a shot and the water pistol is a shonky piece of crap made in China, so no matter how many times he strips that mother down, that thing is never going to hit its target.

EPILOGUE

When I went back over this book, I was surprised by the number of boyfriend references that appear in it, mostly because I have always thought of myself as more 'lonely lady with her good friend booze' than 'woman who is consciously coupled' (TM Gwyneth Paltrow). Certainly that is my public persona. There was even talk of calling this book *Kitty Flanagan: Barren Spinster*, just for a laugh. So out of curiosity, I did the maths (not well obviously) and worked out that over the years I have indeed spent more time single than I have in relationships, and even though I joke about being 'tragically single', there's actually nothing tragic about it. Being single really doesn't bother me at all. And please don't read my tone there as being defensive. I'm not one of those people who gets weirdly aggressive as they try to convince you that they are happy being single, saying things like, 'Being single is better, it's heaps better, everyone should be single. My life is actually better *because* I'm single, I'm totally happy being single!'

What I'm trying to say is, being single is fine, it's absolutely fine. I think too many people still see it as an affliction, something you need to get over and remedy by finding a partner. That mindset certainly explains the proliferation and success of internet-dating sites, all offering to fix the 'problem' of you being single. I've definitely been a lot unhappier in the wrong relationships than I ever have been as a single person. Sure, I went through a slightly unhinged period in my late thirties and early forties but I hope I have explained all that.

Despite my measured rationale of single life, I also understand that humans are social creatures and that everyone gets lonely on occasion and sometimes it can be hard coming home to an empty house. Other times it can be fabulous, and sometimes it just is what it is. The point is there are no absolutes.

And that brings me to pets. Pets have made a huge difference to my life. Having pets has meant I never find myself sitting around at home feeling lonely or unloved or wallowing in self-pity. It is impossible to feel lonely with a purring cat on your lap, and you cannot wallow in anything when there's a dog trailing you around the house, constantly letting you know that he is up for whatever you want to do—hang out, go for a walk, grab a coffee, just so long as he gets to be in your orbit, he's happy.

I could write a whole book about my dog but I won't because it would be dull and not funny. It would just be page after page about how much I love him and how sometimes I cry when I think about the day he's going to die. Which, by the way, is ridiculous because he is neither ill nor elderly, but not so ridiculous if you've read this book and know how easily I burst into tears. I couldn't write a book about my cat but only because it's beyond words how much I love him. Awwww. That's another thing that makes me cry, by the way, when I sit around and 'Sophie's Choice' myself. Which means contemplating which pet I would choose, my cat or my dog, if something terrible happened and I had to pick only one. It might surprise you to know that I pretty much always choose the cat. Simply because he came first. Please don't tell the dog.

And now for the twist in the tale. I ask that you don't tell anyone there is a twist because there is nothing worse than knowing a book has a twist. It means you spend the entire time reading thinking, Ooh, is this the twist? I think this is the twist everyone talked about . . . Oop, no, hang on, *this* is the twist. Yes, this is definitely the twist, or wait a minute . . . maybe *this* is the twist.

Anyway, the twist in this story is that, of course, once I embraced my singleness so wholeheartedly, I met someone (not on the internet) and very unexpectedly found myself in a relationship. Of course, with my track record, this may not still be the case by the time of publication. But for now, at the time of writing, I am dating a cleanskin man (seriously, he is completely free of tattoos despite the fact that he works in the circus, where 'ink' seems mandatory). Not only that, we travel well together, he is patient and funny, he also thinks I'm funny (big tick) *and* he likes talking about his feelings, just like a lady does! In short, he is a unicorn and I plan to keep him for a while. Obviously we'll break up when I need some new material.

ACKNOWLEDGEMENTS

To all the ladies at Allen & Unwin, I have enjoyed my time in the book publishing world immensely. It's such a pleasant work environment—and one that seems to be dominated by women—I wonder if there's a connection? Thank you to Kelly Fagan, who so patiently dragged this book out of me. And to Angela Handley, who was an absolute saint about my never-ending requests for both major and minor changes right until the very end. And to Louise Thurtell—thank you for your constant encouragement (not to mention your relaxed attitude to my missing deadlines) and also for being the person who actually managed to convince me to do this book in the first place.

To my first reader, Bex, thank you so much. Your enthusiasm and genuine support for this book in its early stages is the only reason anyone else ever got to see it. You are truly an amazing friend.

To my second reader, Penny, thank you for the brutal and much-needed editing, and for helping me 'get the clown out of the way' and just tell the story. Also for sitting next to me on planes and in hotels and in dressing rooms playing the 'what are you laughing at now' game. I literally couldn't have done this book without you.

A huge thank you to Tohby Riddle for the beautiful and witty illustrations that help make this book just a little bit classy.

To Artie Laing, you are absolutely one of a kind. I'm so lucky to have you as a manager. And to Karen at A-List, thank you so much for always looking out for me, taking care of me and putting up with me.

Thank you to Rebecca Bana for the beautiful cover photo—you are the only photographer who can make me not hate having my photo taken.

A big thanky face to Bruce Griffiths for always being at the other end of the email whenever I need an expert opinion.

Thanks, too, to my dad for setting such a fine example in life and showing me that you don't have to have a 'real job', that it's possible to work in the arts and do what you love for a living.

Mostly, I want to say thanks to my marmee for always making me want to work harder and be better. I love you and I promise I will try to swear less on stage in future.

And for anyone I've ever been out with—I'm sorry.